GIVING UP THE GHOST

MY 13-YEAR JOURNEY WITH GHOSTS, GEAR, AND GETTING OUT

By Michael J. Baker

First Edition

Cover design by Michael J. Baker
Edited by Cynthia Gangichiodo & Aline Pause Baker

This is a work of nonfiction. Events, locations, and individuals are
portrayed as accurately as memory, records, and editorial clarity
allow. To protect the privacy of individuals, some names, locations,
and identifying details have been changed. Any errors of fact are
the author's alone.

PIERIAN SPRING
PUBLISHING

www.givinguptheghostbook.com
ISBN: 979-8-9998471-0-2

Printed and bound in the United States by
Ingram Spark

This book—and the many years of experience behind it—is dedicated to my incredible friends and family for their constant support, and to my father, James Simon Baker.

Thank you, Dad, for the happiness, the love, and the quiet inspiration that shaped everything I've done.

"Bye for now."

CONTENTS

INTRODUCTION

A WORLD OUT OF FOCUS

For more than a decade, I searched in the dark. Not always metaphorically. Many of my nights were spent in the shadows of abandoned hospitals, basements, barns, and bedrooms—chasing down cold spots and camera blips, decoding whispers that might have been voices and might have been wind. I wasn't alone. Like thousands of others, I was pulled into a subculture that has steadily grown from fringe curiosity to mainstream fascination: the world of paranormal investigation.

This book isn't a ghost story, though it contains many. It's not a believer's memoir or a skeptic's manifesto. It's the story of how I got in, what I saw, what I learned—and why I got out.

You won't find a grand reveal or a final confrontation with the unexplained. What you'll find instead is something quieter and, arguably, more important: a search for truth in a space where truth is often the first casualty. What began as an open-minded quest to explore the possibility of something beyond this world gradually became an exercise in restraint, in science, in ethics, and ultimately, in letting go of comforting ideas in favor of uncomfortable facts. Those facts were everywhere—if you knew how to look.

Why Write This Now?

The paranormal field today is unrecognizable from what it was when I began. Reality TV has transformed ghost hunting into entertainment. Equipment once considered experimental is now merchandised like action figures. Terms like "*EMF spike*" and "spirit box session" are tossed around as if they are established scientific procedures—when most of the time they aren't.

There are well-meaning people in this space. Many. I was one of them. This is not a hit piece on believers, nor a smug take-down of curiosity. What it is, however, is a reckoning. A reflection on how quickly the pursuit of knowledge can be derailed by the need to feel something—anything—extraordinary.

People come to this field for different reasons. Some are grieving. Some are curious. Some are chasing meaning. I came in because I wanted to know if the stories were true. Not just the ones in books or on television, but the ones told in whispers: a cold breath in an empty room, a shadow in the hallway, a voice on the recorder that wasn't there a moment before. I wanted answers. What I found, more often than not, were theatrics disguised as evidence, hope disguised as data, and assumptions disguised as research. The hardest part? I participated in it. At least at the beginning.

A Culture of Confirmation

If you've never been part of a ghost investigation, let me set the stage. There's a rhythm to it: someone reports strange activity—lights flickering, footsteps in the attic, a presence felt but not seen. An investigation is scheduled. A team arrives in matching T-shirts and hauling cases of equipment. Cameras are set up. Audio recorders placed. EM field meters lined up on windowsills. And then, the waiting begins. Darkness. Silence. A whispered question to the void.

"Is anyone here with us?"

A minute passes. Maybe two. Then the meter spikes. Or a pop is heard down the hall. Or a recorder captures a faint syllable. It's enough. Heads nod. Eyes widen. The haunting has begun. But did it? The leap between reaction and interpretation is instantaneous in this field. And it's this leap— the one from unexplained to paranormal—that drives everything. A bump in the night is never just a bump. It's a message. A presence. Proof. Except it rarely is. That's the core problem, and the engine of this book: the lure of evidence that reinforces belief instead of challenging it. It began differently, but it didn't take long to drift.

The Gear That Became Gospel

Much of that drift came in the form of gadgets. The K-II meter. The Ovilus. Spirit boxes. Motion detectors. Flashlights twisted until the filament just barely connects—so that when it flickers, it looks like communication.

I've worked with them all. Tested many. Disassembled others. What I found was rarely paranormal, but almost always revealing. About how people think. About how belief is built. About how easy it is to see what we want to see—especially when the tools themselves are designed to encourage it.

Some devices are honest in their marketing: *"for entertainment purposes only."* But once that label peels off, the claims begin to grow. I've seen investigators swear that a word from the Ovilus confirmed a death that happened decades earlier. I've seen EM field meters interpreted as literal ghost detectors. I've seen cheap radios passed off as portals to the afterlife. Perhaps most troubling of all, I've seen clients in real distress—terrified homeowners—manipulated by teams wielding these devices like instruments of authority. It was enough to make me rethink everything I was doing and, eventually, to stop.

A Story In Three Movements

This book unfolds in three movements. The first explores the world I stepped into, full of enthusiasm and curiosity. It covers the rise of popular ghost hunting, the tools that defined it, and the teams I worked with. It highlights my early investigations, the people I met, and the moments—both exciting and embarrassing—that shaped my approach.

The second movement dives deeper. Here I began building my own equipment, driven by a need for clarity that the off-the-shelf gadgets couldn't provide. I collaborated with engineers, experimented with sensors, and tested claims with as much scientific rigor as I could manage in a dimly lit, often chaotic environment. This section is about trying to do it right—and discovering how rarely that happens.

The final movement is reflection. Why the field couldn't evolve. Why even good-faith efforts to bring science into ghost hunting often fell flat. Why I ultimately walked away. And what I think others—both believers and skeptics—can learn from the time I spent there. It's not just a story about ghosts. It's a story about belief. About human perception. About the intoxicating pull of mystery, and the toll it can take on those who chase it too long.

What This Book Is Not

This is not a catalog of haunted locations. You won't find extended scene-setting of decrepit asylums or long, moody tours of old hotels. You also won't find the kind of hyperbolic language common to the genre: *"demonic presence," "portal to hell,"* or *"residual energy of tragic death."* Not because I never encountered those phrases, but because I refuse to use them without evidence. And that's the point.

In a field built almost entirely on anecdote, drama, and repetition, I wanted to offer something different. A slow, deliberate, sometimes uncomfortable examination of what actually happens on investigations—and why so many of the *"answers"* offered by paranormal investigators don't hold up under scrutiny.

Why It Still Matters

You might ask: Why bother writing this? Why shine a light on the flaws of a field most people dismiss as fantasy anyway? Because some people don't dismiss it. In fact, belief in ghosts is on the rise. So is the monetization of that belief. From TikTok seances to overnight live-streams, from ghost hunting tours to multi-season reality shows, the paranormal is bigger business than ever. And with that growth comes responsibility. Responsibility to think clearly. To question claims. To protect vulnerable people from being misled. To understand the difference between possibility and proof.

I believe curiosity is a virtue. I believe mystery has a place in life. But I also believe that belief without boundaries—without self-examination, without critical thought—can become dangerous. Especially when it's dressed up in gear and sold as research. So this is my way of drawing a line. Of saying: I was there. I saw the gear. I used the tools. I asked the questions. And what I found wasn't a ghost. It was something else entirely.

Authors Note

This book tells the story in words, but some of the moments live on in film and photographs. To explore videos and images connected to the investigations, research and chapters that follow, visit: **www.givinguptheghostbook.com***.*

CHAPTER ONE

RESTLESS ENOUGH TO TRY

In 2005, my life bore little resemblance to what it would become. A different address. A different job. Even a different marriage. On paper, things were steady—predictable, even. But beneath that surface, a quiet sense of unease had begun to settle in. I worked as an electronics engineer and spent my weekends filming weddings—a side hustle that paid just well enough to matter, but never quite enough to change anything. I wasn't in crisis. I wasn't lost. But I wasn't moving forward, either. The days blurred together. The routines became rote. I was, in the truest sense, adrift.

It was early spring in New England—the kind that drags its heels, where the snow has melted but the warmth hasn't yet arrived. The air was damp, the skies gray, the light thin. Work had slowed, and the phone wasn't ringing much. With time suddenly on my hands, a question emerged—quiet at first, then louder: What if I made a film? Not a scripted production, not fiction. A documentary. The kind of project that wouldn't just fill time, but might actually mean something. About a subject I had never quite shaken: ghosts.

Since childhood, the idea of the paranormal had hovered in the margins of my imagination—not as belief, necessarily, but as curiosity. A fascination with what people think they see, with what they're so certain they've felt, with the stories they whisper after dark. I wasn't sure where the path would lead. I just knew I was restless enough to follow it.

Paranormal investigation had, by then, become a pop culture phenomenon. Television was saturated with it. Ghost Hunters, Most Haunted, Paranormal State—all tapping into the public's enduring hunger for the mysterious and unexplained.

As a kid, I'd always imagined ghost hunters as scientists—real scientists. The sort who wore white lab coats, spoke in careful technical terms, and handled equipment you wouldn't find in a Radio Shack. I thought of them as scholars, methodical and precise, probably working out of university labs or obscure government offices. But the ghost hunters on TV were nothing like that. They were regular guys—plumbers by day, paranormal investigators by night—trading spectral theories in the dark with handheld gadgets and night vision cameras. Watching them, I felt something unexpected: possibility. If they could do it, why couldn't I?

At first, the idea was modest. I thought I'd make a short film—fifteen, twenty minutes at most. A side project to sharpen my editing skills, maybe scratch a creative itch. But what began as a casual experiment turned into something else entirely: a multi-year pursuit that would not only consume much of my time, but fundamentally shift the way I saw the paranormal—and the people who claimed to chase it.

The first challenge was access. Paranormal investigators weren't exactly easy to find. Until that point, I'd only encountered them through a television screen. My earliest memories went back to the late '80s and early '90s—segments on *Unsolved Mysteries*, *In Search Of*, even a show called '*That's Incredible*'.

One particular episode of *That's Incredible* had lodged itself in my mind for years: a haunting in a California *Toys 'R' Us*, investigated by a paranormal research team armed with cameras, instruments, psychics and a certainty that something inexplicable was at play.

I must've been nine or ten, but I never forgot it. Still, as I grew older, I started to wonder whether those people were even real. Were paranormal investigators actual professionals or just characters created for TV? If they did exist, I assumed they were rare—maybe part of some credentialed society I'd never heard of. I was wrong. On several counts.

When it came time to find subjects for the film, the solution felt obvious—Craigslist. In the early 2000s, it was the Internet's largest informal gathering space: part marketplace, part message board, part digital Wild West. I posted a simple ad in the "Gigs" section:

Independent filmmaker seeks paranormal investigation team willing to be filmed for documentary project.

I didn't expect much. I was, after all, just a guy with a camera and a vague idea. Why would anyone take me seriously? But within days, my inbox overflowed. Messages poured in from ghost hunters, demonologists, psychic mediums, self-proclaimed exorcists—even a witches coven.

Investigators from Maine to Pennsylvania offered to let me tag along on their cases. It was more than I could have hoped for. More than I could even organize. What I had stumbled into—accidentally, almost naively—was a hidden world. A sprawling, loosely connected network of people who spent their nights chasing shadows and whispering into the dark. And they weren't just characters from television. They were real. Eager. And everywhere.

The first group I chose called themselves the Long Island Society for Paranormal Research, or LISPR—an acronym that immediately struck me as belonging more to a government agency than a group of amateur ghost hunters. Acronyms, I quickly learned, were standard fare in the paranormal community, often emblazoned proudly on matching shirts in dramatic fonts, a visual shorthand for legitimacy.

LISPR invited me to join them for an investigation at the Martin House Restaurant in Provincetown, Massachusetts, a place thick with history. Perched near the tip of Cape Cod, the building purportedly served as a station along the Underground Railroad, sheltering escaped slaves en route to freedom.

Local legend held that those restless souls lingered in the shadows, manifesting as faint footsteps in empty rooms, silverware rattling without cause, and place settings subtly rearranging themselves when no one was watching. It was precisely the kind of layered, evocative setting I had envisioned when starting my documentary. And so, on a spring afternoon, I made a five-hour journey to Provincetown with my friend Anthony Monti, who volunteered as my sound technician and logistical support.

Neither of us knew quite what to expect, having absorbed most of our paranormal knowledge from television: grainy night-vision footage, tense whispers, blurred shadows at the edges of frames—an edited suspense that surely differed from reality.

We arrived at dusk to find Dan, a LISPR team member, waiting beside his car. We exchanged quick pleasantries, then swiftly set about unloading our respective equipment.

Inside, our anticipation gave way almost immediately to disappointment. The restaurant manager, instead of assisting our search for subtlety and quiet, had turned the investigation into a casual gathering, inviting friends who treated the evening as an impromptu social event. Their conversations and laughter resonated loudly through the old building, creating an insurmountable obstacle to the focused silence required by serious paranormal researchers.

Undeterred—or perhaps merely committed to their rituals—the LISPR investigators carried on, setting cameras at precise angles, measuring ambient electromagnetic fields, and whispering instructions over walkie-talkies. Their practiced calm and structured routines belied an obvious frustration simmering just below the surface. Apologies were frequent, earnest assurances that tonight's chaos was atypical. I believed them.

Hours dragged on without incident. No mysterious footsteps disturbed the din, no spectral figures appeared in the darkened hallways. Our recordings captured nothing beyond muffled laughter and ambient noise spilling from the nearby dining area. By midnight, a shared acknowledgment passed among us without words: the night was lost.

Driving back home, the silence wasn't just from fatigue— it was the silence of people trying not to admit they were disappointed. Yet amid that quiet disappointment emerged something unexpected—a sharpened curiosity. The gap between my initial expectations and the messy reality of amateur ghost hunting fascinated me. This first attempt had shown me something vital: the complexity wasn't in the phenomena, but in the people themselves—their motivations, their failings, their beliefs.

Just over a week later, the LISPR team invited me to their next investigation—a place called the S.K. Pierce Mansion in Gardner, Massachusetts. At the time, few outside the local area had ever heard of it.

Today, it's one of the most publicized paranormal hotspots in New England, drawing investigators from across the country who pay for the privilege of wandering its darkened halls. And yes—for the curious—it eventually made an appearance on Ghost Hunters.

The mansion was an imposing Second Empire Victorian: all sharp roof lines, sun-bleached grandeur, and the kind of architectural decay that seemed to breathe mystery. The moment I saw it, I thought: This is it. This is what a haunted house is supposed to look like. Towering, mysterious, and brimming with the weight of history. Honestly, it looked like it had stepped straight out of a Shirley Jackson novel—House on Haunted Hill by way of New England rot.

S.K. Pierce Mansion in Gardner, MA. 2005

The owner, Mark Veau, was a local radio DJ with a perfect broadcaster's voice—smooth, rich, confident. He'd bought the mansion for a fraction of its value, just a few hundred thousand, and ran a tiny British craft shop with his wife out of the front parlor. A 26-room mansion for the price of a starter home. But the deal came with a catch: the place was falling apart. There was a hole in the roof large enough for pigeons to nest on the third floor.

Despite the structural wear, the craftsmanship inside was astonishing. Rich paneling of exotic wood wrapped the halls. Intricately carved details adorned nearly every room. And then there were the fireplaces—thirteen of them—imported Italian marble, standing like ancient relics in rooms now layered with dust and time. The bones of the house were extraordinary, even if the skin was starting to fail.

Mark loved telling stories. About the mansion. Its former residents. Its rumored hauntings. Some of it was likely true. Some, I suspected, was performance. But he delivered it all with such enthusiasm that it didn't seem to matter. Maybe that enthusiasm was part of what transformed the house into the ghost-hunting destination it would eventually become.

For this investigation, I brought along two friends—Joanne and Craig—to help with sound and a second camera. Once again, the LISPR team ran a tight operation. Cameras were placed with intent. Sight lines debated. Equipment double-checked. They weren't winging it. They had a system.

However, amid all the technology and organization, one item they brought along caught my eye and piqued my interest: a plunger. Certainly not something anyone would expect on such an outing. According to Peter Franz, the team leader, it was meant as an homage to the famous television plumbers-turned-paranormal investigators. Silly me—I'd assumed they'd just been dealing with a lot of bad plumbing.

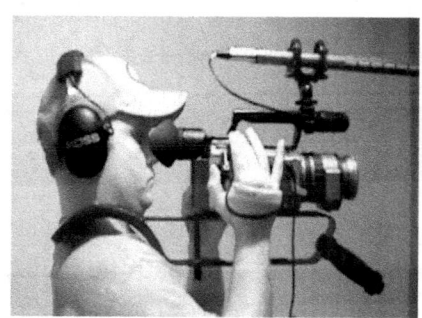

Michael Baker filming at
S.K. Pierce Mansion. 2005

Their toolkit combined consumer electronics and repurposed gear: EM field meters, digital voice recorders, thermometers, night-vision camcorders, and the now-iconic K-II meter—originally built to detect electrical faults but, thanks to television and popular belief, recast as a sort of spiritual Geiger counter.

As night fell, the lights went out. Standard practice, I was told. Still, I found myself quietly questioning it. If the goal was to see something, wouldn't it make sense to leave the lights on? Darkness, it seemed to me, invited more error than clarity. But maybe that was the point. Maybe the darkness wasn't just about conditions—it was about atmosphere. Fear. Immersion. Drama. Whatever the reason, this was their world, and in their world, ghost hunting happened in the dark.

They conducted EVP (*Electronic Voice Phenomena*) sessions, asking questions into the silence and hoping to capture replies on playback. They held up their K-II meters, watching for flashes of orange or red as signs of "*yes*" or "*no*" answers. Occasionally, the lights flickered. More often, they didn't.

To my eyes, the flickers felt random—visual noise in an unpredictable environment. But to the team, each one had weight. They treated every spike, every sound, every drop in temperature with care, as though it might be a signal breaking through the static.

To be fair, they didn't leap blindly. They did try to rule out natural causes. But when no explanation was immediately clear, the default response was to call it evidence and move on. I always sensed they were more invested in confirmation than in debunking. Then again, maybe I was predisposed to skepticism. What they found compelling rarely impressed me. Maybe my expectations were simply too high.

Later, as we reviewed the audio recordings, they pointed out faint voices and distant noises—interpreting them with conviction. I heard them too. But to me, they could have been anything: a shoe scraping the floor, a breath too close to the mic, a car rolling by somewhere in the distance. In the world of audio, ambiguity is easy to find—and harder to dismiss.

Still, compared to the Martin House, this was a vastly better investigation. It was quieter. More focused. There were moments—brief, ambiguous, easily debated—but moments nonetheless. A distant knock. A spike on a meter. A voice on playback that didn't have an obvious source. Each one made you pause, even if only for a second. But it still wasn't enough.

I wasn't just looking for suggestion—I wanted something definitive. A moment so clear, so visceral, that it couldn't be dismissed. The kind of moment that anchors a story. The kind that changes people's minds. On the long, quiet drive home, windshield streaked with the light of passing highway signs, I made a decision: I wouldn't follow just one team. I would follow every lead. Every invitation. Every rumor. Every hallway that might hold a whisper on the other side of the dark. I wasn't done. Not even close.

But before I could dive into the flood of messages waiting in my bloated inbox, I had to face a practical truth: if I wanted the film to reach people outside the paranormal bubble, I needed to give them a way in. A familiar face. A recognizable name. A story they already had a foot in.

Television had become the modern gateway to the paranormal. Like it or not, it shaped the public's understanding of the field. If I wanted the project to resonate—to stretch beyond the already converted—I'd have to walk through that same door.

That meant finding someone known. Someone with visibility. A figure that could serve as a kind of bridge between the insular world I was uncovering and the audience watching from their living rooms. And, to my surprise, I found not one—but two.

Both were well-known in the paranormal community. Both carried weight for entirely different reasons. And both agreed to speak with me.

JOHN ZAFFIS

The first high-profile figure I interviewed was John Zaffis—often referred to, with equal parts reverence and theatrical flair, as The Godfather of the Paranormal. A self-described demonologist and the nephew of Ed and Lorraine Warren, Zaffis had spent decades working in the shadows of their legacy, carving out a space of his own in the paranormal world.

Though he'd made sporadic television appearances—news spots, brief interviews—at the time, Zaffis still occupied a liminal space between underground figure and public personality. He had enough recognition to bridge the gap

between the insular ghost hunting community and a broader audience, and that was exactly what I needed for my film.

For those unfamiliar with the name, Zaffis would later become the star of the History Channel series *The Haunted Collector*, a show

John Zaffis during his interview for
14 Degrees - A Paranormal Documentary.
2006

built around his private museum—a collection of allegedly haunted or possessed objects he claimed to have removed from clients' homes in order to save them from spiritual torment.

I hadn't heard of him before the film, but investigators I spoke with mentioned Zaffis repeatedly—always with reverence and barely contained excitement. He'd been involved in a high-profile possession case in Southington, Connecticut, in the early '90s, which led to the Discovery Channel documentary *A Haunting in Connecticut* and a subsequent dramatized film of the same name. The story clearly endured.

We were invited to conduct our interview at his museum, which turned out to be less 'institution' and more 'converted space in his home.' That in itself was a surprise. After all, if these items were so deeply haunted that they needed to be removed from other people's homes for their safety, why on earth would anyone bring them back to their own?

According to John the items had been ritually *"cleansed"*—neutralized by spiritual ceremonies that stripped them of their attachments. Safe, he assured us.

I can't say I was fully on board. But I wanted to be. I wanted the danger to be real, the rituals to have power, the romanticism of a battle between good and evil to be on display for the all world to see, and I wanted to be the one to get it all on film. Unfortunately, I don't think I ever hit that mark.

What struck me most about Zaffis wasn't just his ease in front of the camera—it was his command of the interview itself. He had a well-practiced rhythm, and a clever conversational trick: he asked himself questions, then answered them before anyone else could.

"Do I believe the house was haunted? Yes."
"Do I think the family was in danger? Absolutely."

It was an effective tactic—one that allowed him to steer the conversation, to frame the story entirely on his own terms. The approach projected authority, confidence. But the more I listened, the more I noticed something else: the details were fluid. Facts shifted. Timelines blurred. Sometimes dates changed slightly or events were condensed—reshaped for clarity, or perhaps drama. It wasn't overt. It wasn't deceptive in the traditional sense. But it was performative. And perhaps most curious of all wasn't what he said, but what he didn't say.

Zaffis carried the title of "*demonologist*," a term that suggests deep knowledge—taxonomy, hierarchy, an academic grasp of malevolent entities. Yet, when it came time to talk specifics about his museum never once did he identify the entities said to be attached to the objects in his collection.

Not by name. Not by class. Not even by general type. The language stayed vague. Generalities were preferred. Labels were mentioned, but rarely explored. I admit, I expected more.

It left me wondering whether the title itself was more useful than the doctrine behind it. After all, demonologist plays well on TV. It reads powerfully on a conference poster. It gives your story an edge. And John Zaffis—media-savvy, camera-ready—knew how to lean into that.

I don't doubt that he's been where he says he's been. The

experiences were likely real to the people involved. But when it came to his own museum—his personal collection—the line between practitioner and performer seemed to blur.

STEVE GONSALVES

Our next high-profile interview was with Steve Gonsalves—one of the core investigators from the television series Ghost Hunters, which was airing at the time on the SyFy Channel.

Steve had been part of the show from the beginning and had become one of the most recognizable faces in modern paranormal media. Reaching out to him felt like a long shot. I contacted his agent with no real expectation of a reply—but to my surprise, he agreed to an interview.

We arranged to film at a hotel in Springfield, Massachusetts—not far from where he lived at the time. I remember standing in that rented room with my small crew, our makeshift backdrop lit and leveled, cameras ready, microphones tested. It was the kind of setup you pull together with just enough gear and not quite enough time—but everything was in place. Then came the knock at the door.

And just like that, it felt as if we'd stepped through the television screen. The man I'd watched for years on late-night cable was suddenly standing in front of me, smiling, shaking hands, stepping into our shot.

Steve was gracious from the start—relaxed, approachable, professional. As we rolled through the interview, he delivered thoughtful, well-paced responses. He knew how to look at the

Michael Baker interviewing Steve Gonsalves for
14 Degrees - A Paranormal Documentary. 2006

camera—or rather away from the camera, when to pause, how
to keep his tone level and clear. He was experienced, media-
trained in the way that only comes from years in front of the
lens.

He spoke confidently about TAPS (*The Atlantic
Paranormal Society*)—the methods, the cases, the things
they'd seen. There was no hesitation. No uncertainty. As he
described his experiences, it was clear: he believed in what
he'd witnessed. And maybe he was right.

He'd seen far more than I had. Investigated the most
notorious locations. Been present for the moments that
inspired thousands of late-night YouTube replays. A part of me
wondered if my skepticism was simply inexperience. Maybe

he had earned that confidence. Maybe you don't ask as many questions when you've already found your answers. But another part of me—the quieter, more cynical part—wondered something else.

Had Steve become, in some ways, a product of the phenomenon he helped shape? Was he still investigating the unknown, or had he become another gear in the machine that turned ghost hunting into entertainment?

During our conversation, he mentioned something that caught me off guard: before Ghost Hunters, Steve had worked as a police officer in Springfield. He'd joined TAPS long before the cameras arrived. He was, in many ways, the real deal—boots on the ground before the bright lights showed up.

And yet, despite the show's early success, I learned that during the first seasons, only the two lead investigators—Jason and Grant—were paid by the network. The rest—including Steve—were essentially volunteers.

Let that sink in: starring in a hit television show, watched by millions each week, and receiving no paycheck. I'd hear similar stories from other investigators later—people whose shows had been green-lit, whose faces had appeared on posters, whose voices narrated dramatic reveals—working for exposure, not income. The show had made them famous. But fame, it turned out, didn't always pay the bills.

Networks, it seemed, believed exposure was payment enough. Fame—however fleeting—was treated as the real currency. The participants were left to figure out how to turn their fifteen minutes into something sustainable. I found that idea absurd. From there, the journey expanded.

Over the next two years, my team – Joanne, Anthony and I—a.k.a *New Gravity Media*—followed dozens of paranormal groups across the Northeast, logging more than 6,000 miles in the process. Nearly every weekend, I found myself somewhere new: basements, attics, long-abandoned hospitals, forgotten cemeteries, roadside motels with sagging roofs and stories that refused to die.

The scientists I had hoped to find—the ones I'd imagined at the start, in lab coats with clipboards and control groups— never showed up. Not once. Not at any of the places we visited. But I wasn't ready to give up. Maybe, I thought, the truth was still out there. Maybe I'd be the one to find it.

Every group we encountered had its own way of chasing shadows. Each had their own hierarchy of belief, their own rituals, their own favored tools. And what became immediately clear was this: no two groups defined *"evidence"* the same way. For some, EVP was the gold standard.

If a voice appeared on playback that hadn't been heard in the moment, that was proof. Others placed their faith in EM field meters, treating every flicker and spike as a sign of presence. Some trusted thermal readings. Some relied solely on instinct—a psychic's impression, a gut feeling, a cold shiver in a room that shouldn't have been cold. What none of them could do was explain why their method was reliable. Or why it should be trusted above another.

There were teams who approached investigations with a kind of ritualized discipline—clipboards in hand, meticulously laid-out gear, structured plans. Others leaned into the metaphysical: pendulums, séances, crystals, and chants. In some cases, it was hard to tell where the investigation ended and the theater began. But across all of it—every location, every method, every team—one thing remained consistent: No one applied a true scientific method.

The deeper I went, the more I realized we weren't just documenting ghost hunts—we were documenting belief systems. Rituals. The quiet desperation of people searching for answers with tools handed to them by self-proclaimed experts and television personalities. Some of those figures were more respected than others. A few had carved out loyal followings within their communities. But none of them were credentialed scientists.

Sure, there were places back then that offered *"certifications"* in psychical research—but those credentials were usually created by the very people offering them. It was a closed loop of self-appointed authority: people who read a few books, watched a few shows, formed some opinions, and emerged as supposed experts in a realm that no edge of science had ever even confirmed—let alone understood.

And yet, nearly every investigation introduced something new: new gadgets, new theories, new contradictions. It was equal parts fascinating and surreal. I saw it all. From DIY tech enthusiasts building blinking, beeping contraptions in their garages to soft-spoken sensitives who claimed they could feel spirits move through them.

Some groups arrived with enough gear to rival a news crew. Others brought nothing but a flashlight and a spiral-bound notebook. But across all that noise, all the contradiction and theater and trial-and-error, there was a common thread—a shared hope. The belief that we don't just disappear. That there's more waiting for us beyond the veil.

THE PREMIERE

As our film —*14 Degrees: A Paranormal Documentary*— neared completion, what had started as a loose, twenty-minute sketch swelled into a two-hour film. It premiered on October 17, 2007, at Showcase Cinemas in Revere, Massachusetts.

The evening felt less like a screening than a convergence: everyone I'd met in the two years prior—through interviews, late-night conversations, shared doubts, small triumphs—was there under a single roof.

Before the film began I gave a speech, and standing in that foyer, facing the room of familiar strangers, it was like stepping into the Twilight Zone. All those strange encounters, small kindnesses, frustrations, and revelations coalesced into one moment. It was surreal and, against every quiet hope that had carried the project this far, deeply fulfilling.

But it didn't feel like closure. More like a pause. I hadn't found what I was looking for—I'd only shown how others were looking. Filming had been the first step. The next step was action.

For two years, I had followed others—capturing their methods, listening to their stories, walking through the spaces they believed held answers. I had watched them chase something just out of reach, and I gave them a voice.

Now it was time to stop following—and start building. I wasn't looking for legends anymore. I wasn't interested in secondhand tales. I wanted to test the boundaries for myself. I wanted to move from shadows to substance. I didn't know if I would find proof. But I knew I would find the truth. Even if the truth wasn't what I expected.

CHAPTER TWO

DIRECTION OF TRUTH

Watching from the sidelines wasn't enough anymore. I wanted to step into the process—to see what happened when the cameras were off, when no one was performing. To do that, I had to join a team. And that's what led me to Boston Paranormal Investigators—BPI. Based in Waltham, Massachusetts, the group was led by Tom Elliott—a straight-talking, no-nonsense investigator who welcomed just about anyone with even a hint of curiosity about the unknown. And when I say anyone, I mean it.

Tom's door was open wider than most in the field. He was sharp. Blunt. Quick with a comeback and quicker to call out nonsense. A Mensa member with a razor-wire intellect, Tom had spent much of his adult life questioning the strange instead of chasing it. Back in the 1980s, he'd even hosted a local cable-access TV show where he explored the unexplained—long before it was trendy, long before ghost hunting became reality-show material.

He wasn't just well-read—he was well-connected. He counted people like Lorraine Warren and Betty Hill as casual friends. In the world of the paranormal, those names carried weight. Legends, depending on who you asked. But to Tom, they were just part of the story. He used to tell us about UFO-watching trips with Betty in Exeter, New Hampshire—nights spent staring at the sky, waiting for something to move.

His stories weren't showy. They weren't told for applause. It wasn't name-dropping. That was just his life. Strange, storied, and unapologetically curious.

What set Tom apart, though, was his approach. He didn't believe everything he heard—but he didn't dismiss everything either. He listened. He questioned. And somewhere between those two poles—between skepticism and wonder—was where he made his home. Unlike so many self-appointed gatekeepers in the paranormal world, Tom didn't cling to exclusivity. He wasn't interested in hierarchies or credentials. His philosophy was disarmingly simple: Every voice mattered. Every perspective had value. The result was a revolving door of some of the most fascinating, bizarre, and unforgettable people I've ever encountered.

BPI wasn't like the matching-shirt groups with rigid hierarchies—though at times, I sensed they might have liked that sort of recognition. In truth, it was closer to a weekly book club—only instead of novels, we pored over case studies, EVP recordings, and the big, unanswered questions that kept people coming back. *What happens when we die? What do we mean when we say "energy"? Why do some people experience hauntings and others don't?*

Every meeting was a cocktail of perspectives. Some members clung tightly to scientific principles—insisting on control groups, environmental baselines, repeatable data. Others leaned fully into the metaphysical: chakra alignments, psychic impressions, past-life memories.

Debates were common. Sometimes heated. Sometimes stubbornly silent. But whether you were a physicist or a medium—or just someone trying to make sense of a personal experience—you had a seat at the table. And that was the beauty—and the chaos—of an open-door policy.

You never knew who would walk in next. One night, it might be a retired police officer with a story he couldn't explain. Another night, a soft-spoken psychic claiming to communicate with the dead since childhood. Occasionally, people came just to observe—curious, cautious, unsure if they even belonged. And then there were the others. The ones who tested the limits of belief—and sometimes, reality.

I'll never forget the man who walked in clutching a crumpled paper bag filled with loose documents and grainy photographs. He claimed—without hesitation or irony—that he had irrefutable proof of his own alien abduction. More than that, he insisted that everyone he'd ever told about it had mysteriously vanished.

He spoke with a kind of frantic gravity, as if just saying the words aloud put all of us in danger. His hands trembled as he rifled through the papers, eyes darting to the windows as if expecting someone—or something—to be watching. And just as quickly as he arrived, he was gone. We never saw him again. But that was Boston Paranormal. That was the magic—and the madness. It was unpredictable. It was messy. It was alive. And it was exactly what I needed.

Even if many of the investigations we conducted felt more like haunted house tours than scientific endeavors, BPI gave me something no other team had: a glimpse into the living side of this work. The human side. The stories, the motives, the fears, and the fragile hope that maybe—just maybe—we're not alone. And in the end, that was just as valuable as any data point. My time with Boston Paranormal began during the filming of *14 Degrees* and continued long after the final credits rolled. In fact, I was one of the group's original members.

What drew me in—and kept me coming back—wasn't just the investigations. It was the open-mindedness. The willingness to explore ideas without ego or ridicule. That rare balance between curiosity and critical thinking. It was that mindset that led my production team and me to stage one of our most talked-about on-screen experiments: a test involving the infamous Ouija board.

OUIJA: YES OR NO

The premise was simple: *Do Ouija boards actually do anything?* Rather than testing it ourselves—where our own skepticism might cloud the results—we decided it would be more compelling to hand the process over to people who fully believed. People who not only trusted in the board's power but claimed to be able to produce results when using it.

Jim Bucknam, a fellow Boston Paranormal member and self-described psychic medium and exorcist, helped us locate one of our participants: Barbara Szafranski, a well-known psychic and the proprietor of Angelica of the Angels, a metaphysical shop in Salem, Massachusetts. The second participant, "*Holly*," was recommended by my production team member Anthony.

We staged the experiment at Tom Elliott's house, which also served as the unofficial headquarters for BPI. We'd held countless meetings there, debated everything from EVP classification to haunted mirrors. It felt like the right place to see if the board could live up to its reputation.

I've always been skeptical of Ouija boards. But like tarot cards, pendulums, and other divinatory tools, they intrigue me. Not because I believe they work—but because I've always been fascinated by how much they rely on interpretation. And interpretation is susceptible to bias. It's difficult—sometimes impossible—to separate what might be coming through from what the users are simply projecting.

Over the years, I'd heard countless stories. Ouija sessions that led to strange events: flickering lights, cold spots, sudden knocks, unexplained messages. Even possession.

I'd spoken with investigators who refused to go near the boards, calling them reckless, dangerous, even evil. Some insisted that using one was tantamount to flinging open a spiritual doorway to hell with no way to close it—a direct invitation for something dark to step through. So going in, we certainly didn't know what to expect.

Privately, I hoped for something—anything—that might challenge my skepticism. Not because I wanted to believe, necessarily, but because I wanted to be wrong. I wanted something real. Something that couldn't be brushed off as coincidence or psychology. Something that left a mark. And if there was any truth to the claims surrounding Ouija boards, this setup gave us a fair chance at finding it.

Both of our participants believed deeply in the process. One was a practicing psychic medium. The other had spent years using the board in private sessions. We imposed no restrictions. No scripts. No controls. Whatever rituals or techniques they felt were necessary, they were free to use. This was their domain. We were simply there to observe and document.

To capture the session, we used three cameras: two stationary, and one handheld—my job—to follow any subtle movements or unexpected phenomena. A thermometer was placed nearby to monitor temperature changes. An EM field meter was positioned on the table to track any electromagnetic fluctuations that might occur during the session. We were as prepared as we could be. Now all we needed was something to happen.

At the time, I knew almost nothing about EM field meters. I couldn't have told you whether a reading was meaningful, misleading, or completely irrelevant like most of us in BPI. Placing that meter was simply mimicry. It was what I'd seen on television—call it procedural performance. Set the gear.

Monitor the space. Hope something happens. And if something had happened? My interpretation would've been pure guesswork. Still, the setup felt responsible. Like we were doing our due diligence, even if we didn't fully understand the tools.

Once everything was in place, we dimmed the lights. Our two participants took their positions, fingers gently on the planchette. The rest of us—Boston Paranormal members, my

Barbara Szafranski, Tom Elliot, and Holly during the Ouija board experiment. Filmed for *14 Degrees - A Paranormcl Documentary* in 2006

production crew—sat silently around the room. Cameras rolled. Notebooks ready. Every breath and movement documented.

For the first few minutes, nothing happened. Questions were asked into the stillness, and the stillness answered back with silence. But then, around the ten-minute mark, the planchette began to move. It wasn't spelling anything—not names, not numbers, not yes or no. Just slow, drifting motions across the board.

Whether it was unconscious muscle movement or something more who can say. That's always the problem with Ouija boards: intention and projection become indistinguishable.

Barbara, eyes closed, seemed to enter a kind of trance. She was the one speaking—the one asking questions. Holly kept her fingers on the planchette, her gaze fixed on Barbara, almost like she was waiting for direction. It was clear who was in control. Then something strange happened—not paranormal, necessarily, but undeniably odd.

The planchette began tracing wide, deliberate circles. At first, slowly. Then faster. Then, without any hesitation, the board itself was removed from the table altogether—and the participants continued moving the planchette in those same circles directly on the tabletop. Fingers still tight. Motion uninterrupted.

It's important to keep in mind that based on the accepted, and expected operation of this board we are supposed to simply accept that the planchette was moving independent of the users will. That these fast concentric circles are not Barbara or Holly's doing, but rather the mysterious entity they have channeled. I was not sold.

At this point Barbara shifted fully into channeling. The board was no longer needed. She began speaking aloud the answers she claimed were coming through. The Ouija session had transformed into something entirely different—something more performative, less structured. She had entered full 'medium' mode.

I kept the handheld camera trained on their faces. Holly

looked lost, bored almost—her hands still moving, but her expression vacant. Passive. Barbara, by contrast, was fully in control. Eyes closed, voice steady, presence commanding.

Whatever this was, it was hers now. And then—just as the session seemed to reach its peak—I heard something behind me. A sound, a thud, a moan from the hallway. Anthony leaned over and whispered, "*Look at Jim.*" I turned.

Jim Bucknam—BPI's psychic medium—was hunched near the front door, his body tense, fists clenched at his sides like he was fighting off a seizure. A moment later, he straightened, eyes wide and wild, and suddenly slammed himself against the door. He shouted—loud, urgent, theatrical:

> "*No! You're not coming through me!*
> *You do not speak through my voice!*"

My team and I looked at each other. Whether or not the Ouija board had worked suddenly felt irrelevant. We had a moment. We had something. Jim Bucknam's alleged possession lasted nearly twenty minutes—bursts of shouting, muttering, sudden contortions, long silences snapped by panic. It was intense, uncomfortable, and undeniably dramatic.

By the time the Ouija session in the other room ended, Jim had collapsed onto the stairs. His face was wet with sweat. He rocked slightly, repeating the same words over and over:

> "*I just want to go home. I just want to go home.*"

I didn't blame him. So did I. But at the time, I still had a film to finish. Whether this house had played host to an authentic paranormal disturbance, a spontaneous psychodrama, or something stranger still was hard to say. All I knew for sure was this: the line between belief and performance had just gotten a little blurrier.

To me—and I'll stress that this is just my opinion—the whole evening felt like a tug-of-war between two psychics, each trying to out-do the other for attention.

Of course, I'll never know for certain. Maybe Jim truly was under spiritual attack, the unintended target of something stirred up by an unstable Ouija session. But from where I sat, it looked like he realized Barbara wasn't producing anything all that compelling—and decided to take over. Maybe I'm wrong. But I'm also not afraid to say that the entire event felt off the rails.

Whatever the truth was, it reminded me of something essential: in paranormal research, you're not just studying the unexplained. You're studying people. And people—believers, skeptics, investigators, psychics—bring their stories, their motives, and their baggage with them.

THE ADVENTURE CONTINUES

In the months that followed—and long after the completion of *14 Degrees*—I continued working with Boston Paranormal. I even followed Jim on several of the house clearings and so-called exorcisms he performed.

Jim had a vast network of connections and was often

invited into homes where the residents believed they were under spiritual siege. They described oppressive presences, strange disturbances, feelings of dread. Jim's solution was a process he called '*clearing*,' and it involved what he referred to as the '*Mansions of Light*' or '*Mansions of God*'—a council of deities and spiritual figures he claimed to summon for assistance.

The roster was eclectic, to say the least. Jesus Christ. The Great White Buffalo. Archangels. Animal spirits. Sometimes ancestral guides. According to Jim, these entities would confront and remove the malevolent presence, banishing it to a place where it could no longer affect the physical world.

He believed they were sealed away behind what he called D-sharp shields—seven of them, in fact. A kind of vibrational barrier tied to the musical note D-sharp.

It was, as he described it, a harmonic lock. I'll be honest—I never fully understood how that was supposed to work. The explanation straddled a line between mystical philosophy and science fiction. But on the nights I joined him, I wasn't there to interrogate. I was there to observe.

Jim insisted the process was physically taxing. That it drained his energy, sometimes leaving him nauseous, dizzy, emotionally spent. And maybe it did. I've said it before and I'll say it again: I can't know what's happening inside someone else's mind or body. But I remained—quietly, respectfully—skeptical.

Over time, the membership of Boston Paranormal Investigators shifted. Some of the original diehards remained, while new, enthusiastic members came and went. It was fascinating to watch how differently people approached the same pursuit—each with their own beliefs, rituals, and investigative styles.

I appreciated the diversity of thought, but if I'm being honest, my attention was drifting elsewhere. The Ouija board experiment had lit a spark. That kind of inquiry—structured, however imperfect—was what excited me. It scratched a different itch. So while others chased cold spots or EVP, I began quietly working behind the scenes, trying to build something of my own. Tools, devices—anything that could help me test claims in a more controlled, measurable way.

I'll be the first to admit: I had no idea what I was doing. Honestly, I still don't. But I figured that if I could build devices to record even basic environmental data, I might start to identify patterns. And if patterns existed, maybe they could point to something real. Something repeatable. Something worth chasing.

FOR THE RECORD

Thinking like an electronics engineer, I started with what I understood: power. Most of the gear we used was battery-operated. So I began by focusing on voltage—specifically, the subtle fluctuations that powered the sensors and displays. After all, those voltages were directly proportional to the environmental elements that the devices were designed to measure.

My idea was simply to record voltage changes with timestamps. Then compare those readings to other environmental observations—temperature shifts, unexplained sounds, or anomalies.

Instead of relying on blinking lights and gut feelings, I could begin collecting real-time data, and maybe, just maybe, a pattern would emerge. Or at the very least, I could start separating signal from noise.

I didn't have a lab. No funding. Just a soldering iron, a multimeter, and a growing list of questions. But for the first time since I began this journey, I felt like I was moving toward something more than storytelling. I wasn't just chasing shadows anymore—I was trying to measure them.

The first step was to find a data logger capable of recording extremely small voltage changes. Working with such precision was vital to any plausible success I might have, so finding the right equipment to work with was crucial.

After some research, I landed on a few models from a company called DATA Q. I could've built something myself, but I was impatient. I didn't want to spend months designing a solution someone else had already solved. These units were affordable, compact, and highly precise—able to record changes as small as 10 microvolts, and log them up to 200 times per second.

To add some context to those values, a *microvolt* is an extremely tiny amount of energy. If we think of voltage like sound volume. One volt is like someone speaking in a normal voice, but a microvolt is like the rustling of a leaf, but you're trying to hear it from across a football field. It's so faint that your ears—or in this case a regular voltmeter—can't pick it up. But these data-logging devices *could*! And even more important, they can save it with a timestamp.

Finding that kind of granularity was a game changer. It would allow me to build sensitive gear to map timelines, sync multiple inputs, and most importantly, ask better questions.

Of course, acquiring the gear was one thing. Applying strict scientific control to the unpredictable, chaotic environment of a field investigation? That was something else entirely. But I wasn't trying to prove anything yet. I was just looking for clues.

The first device I chose to modify was the infamous K-II meter, a small, handheld device with a row of multicolored LED lights that indicate changes in electromagnetic fields. It has a simple on/off button and typically features a gray or black plastic casing shaped like a TV remote.

At the time, it was everywhere. You couldn't watch a ghost hunting show without seeing it front and center, treated like a trusted authority. But from an engineering standpoint, and for the purpose of science based research, it was a joke. It still is. It has no calibrated scale, no digital readout—just six LEDs that lit up in sequence without context. No timestamps. A power button that requires it be continuously pressed in order to work all of which make continuous monitoring a chore unless you physically modified the circuit. Which is exactly why I chose it. A perfect first step.

By wiring my data logger directly into the voltage that powers the LED display, I could record the voltage that is directly proportional to the device readings. Instead of interpreting colored flashes, I could record actual voltage levels—complete with timestamps.

Modified K-II meter with data logging and visual number display.

Suddenly, this over hyped, plastic gadget had the potential to produce data. Maybe useless data. Maybe garbage. But at least it was something I could measure and correlate. And that, for me, changed everything.

Whether or not the K-II was detecting anything paranormal remained to be seen—but for the first time, I had a way to move from anecdote to evidence. And it didn't require eyes on a blinking light or hours of video review. It just worked. The modification only took a couple days, and to their credit, my teammates in Boston Paranormal were genuinely excited.

We brought the rig to several investigations, and it performed exactly as intended—delivering clean, time-stamped logs of every spike the K-II registered. Encouraged by the initial engineering success, I added data-logging capabilities to other devices—temperature sensors, motion detectors, anything we could wire and sync. We carried the setup everywhere, hoping to uncover something concrete. And sure, the K-II registered spikes—just as it was designed to. But that's all it did. It never really offered anything beyond what could be attributed to randomness. Worse, it couldn't tell us why it had spiked.

That was the real issue. The deeper flaw. The K-II—and nearly every other repurposed gadget in the paranormal toolkit—suffered from the same fundamental limitation: it could tell you that something happened, but not what caused it. And in a field built on unexplained phenomena, the *"what"* is everything. It seems I'd just put lipstick on a pig.

Electromagnetic energy is omnipresent. It's in the walls. In the air. In our devices and routers and thermostats. A refrigerator cycling on. A microwave in the next room. A Bluetooth connection. Even a cellphone just checking for a signal can trip a meter. No matter how many lights you add, no matter how dramatic the display—without context, these tools are blind. They can't distinguish between the ordinary and the extraordinary. In a discipline that claims to be investigative, that's a serious problem.

AUTOMATED OBSERVATION

It was clear that if I wanted better answers, I needed better tools. At the time, I didn't know what that would look like—but I knew one thing with certainty: devices like the K-II were useless. If I couldn't say what triggered a spike, then I didn't want to know about it. Without specificity, it was just noise—one more distraction in a field already drowning in ambiguity.

The more I thought about it, the more I realized that a

significant part of that noise came from us—the investigators. Our bodies. Our equipment. Our movements and conversations and unconscious biases.

Every whisper, every shift in a chair, every casual bump against a table added yet another variable to environments we were supposedly trying to study objectively.

I started to wonder: what if the solution wasn't better investigators? What if it was fewer? Or maybe—none at all. What if a device could sit silently in a room, completely unattended, and record relevant environmental data? Something that could monitor motion, temperature fluctuations, audio anomalies—even electromagnetic directionality—without human interference? If I could build a system like that, maybe I could strip away a lot of the human contamination. Remove the observer bias. Reduce the noise. And maybe—just maybe—get closer to the truth.

Of course, I knew that wouldn't solve everything. A machine can't interpret a feeling. It can't assess personal experience. But it would be a step in the right direction. A small step toward credibility.

One of the biggest challenges in paranormal research is the field's reputation for being pseudoscientific—and truthfully, that reputation is often deserved. The broader scientific community ignores the field not because they're afraid of what we might find, but because we rarely produce anything that resembles empirical evidence.

The real barrier isn't belief. It's demonstrability. And that idea—the search for consistent, measurable correlations—is what began driving my work. I wasn't trying to prove the existence of ghosts. I was trying to determine whether anything—anything at all—was happening during these experiences that could be measured, repeated, and eventually understood.

AUDIO DIRECTIONALITY

While I continued wrestling with the limitations of EM field analysis, my attention began to temporarily sideline toward a related question—one that had nagged at me since the very beginning: *What about sound?*

If energy fluctuations and sources could be recorded, what about audio? And more specifically: could we capture not just what was heard—but the direction it came from?

Imagine listening to an audio file and being able to tell what part of the room the sound originated? That could help immensely in the qualification of data as evidence. Directionality, I realized, might be the next frontier. Nearly every group I worked with recorded hours of EVP sessions, hoping to capture disembodied voices or unexplained sounds. But much like EM field readings, the core issue wasn't just contamination—it was source uncertainty.

We rarely knew, and often couldn't know, exactly where a sound had originated. An EVP might show up clearly on a recorder. But was it a voice from the hallway? A whisper from a nearby room? Someone shifting in their chair? A stray breath caught too close to the mic? Most of the time, we were left guessing. And that made the evidence weak at best, misleading at worst.

It seemed obvious to me that if we wanted to treat audio as meaningful data, we needed to track not just what was heard—but where it came from. The source, not the signal. Knowing direction alone could help rule out false positives or identify potentially compelling anomalies. Simple—at least conceptually.

For my proof of concept, I arranged four microphones, each pointing in a different direction—north, south, east, west—alignment to these directions would happen on location.

Each microphone fed into its own small circuit, wired to control a corresponding LED and linked to a four channel data logger. The louder the sound picked up by a mic, the brighter the LED would glow and the higher the voltage recorded.

In theory, the microphone closest to the source of a sound

Electronics inside the prototype version of the audio direction finder.

would generate the highest voltage, producing a visibly brighter LED. That voltage, recorded with a timestamp, would give me not just a moment of interest—but a directional clue.

It wasn't triangulation in the strict acoustic sense, but it didn't need to be. If it worked, it would be simple, readable, and—most importantly—repeatable. That alone made it promising. Not bad for a plastic project box filled with scavenged components.

After running a basic smoke test on my bench at home—clapping from different angles, snapping fingers, shouting into corners—the proof of concept held.

Voltage data was clean, LED behavior was responsive, and the logger recorded without a hitch. It was time for a field test. BPI had just booked a private home investigation in Arlington, MA—scheduled a week or two later. Naturally, I jumped at the chance. The claims from the homeowner were nothing out of the ordinary: vague feelings of unease, brief sightings of a female figure, and—most relevant to my experiment—reports of whispered voices in the bedroom late at night. Exactly the kind of scenario I had hoped for. It was the perfect test-bed for an audio direction finder.

Once the rest of the team had finished setting up their gear in the usual way, I placed my device at the foot of the bed—dead center in the room. I took extra care to align it with proper compass points and assigned each channel on the data logger to a corresponding direction.

When the team called for lights out, I found myself thinking—maybe for the first time—that the darkness might actually help in this particular case. Thanks to the soft red glow of the LEDs, it was immediately obvious which side of the cube was reacting. When a light pulsed, we could tell exactly where the sound had come from. There was no guesswork and at first, it felt like a success.

The cube did exactly what it was built to do. It picked up every sound the team made—spoken commands, claps, knocks—and pointed, without fail, to where the noise came from. That alone felt like a small triumph. But the excitement didn't last long. Just as quickly, it exposed a serious flaw. One I hadn't accounted for. Calibration.

Version 2 of the Audio direction finder. Now featuring advanced analysis and recording. 2013

Each of the cube's four microphones had its own amplifier circuit. On paper, they were identical. Same diagram. Same components. But in practice, they weren't quite the same at all. That's because electronic parts, even fresh out of the package, aren't perfect. Every resistor, capacitor, and transistor has what's called a *"tolerance"*—a tiny range of acceptable error built into how they're manufactured. A resistor marked as 1,000 ohms, for instance, might actually measure 980 or 1,020 and still be considered within spec. That margin, small as it is, added up.

So even though each channel was built to be identical, their sensitivity—the way they picked up and amplified sound—

was slightly off. Channel one wasn't exactly like channel two. Channel two wasn't like channel three. And the result was a cube that could still point to sound, but not with perfect consistency. If it was going to be more than a clever prototype, I'd have to fix that.

When working with sounds at the edge of human hearing— the kind often cited in EVP recordings—those tiny inconsistencies became a real problem. The voltage differences between microphones were so slight, so razor-thin, they could just as easily be blamed on natural quirks in the circuitry as on any actual clue about direction. It meant that what looked like a signal might just be static dressed up as certainty.

The illusion of accuracy was just that—an illusion. Fixing the issue would require research, and likely a full redesign of the amplification stage.

Honestly, I wasn't even sure if the level of precision I needed was possible without super pricey lab-grade equipment. But that didn't matter—not yet. I'd proven the concept, and in a field long dominated by theatrics and speculation, a working concept felt like real progress.

I returned to the drawing board with new purpose. My head was buzzing with ideas—twelve at least—each one aimed at finding just one sliver of the paranormal that could be measured, tested, or demonstrated in a way that could hold up under scrutiny.

REFLECTIONS

Looking back, it was clear how much my time with Boston Paranormal had shaped me. It sharpened my thinking. It forced me to question not only the claims we investigated, but my own assumptions. I had come to understand that paranormal investigation wasn't really about the equipment— or even the evidence.

At its core, it was truly about people. Their stories. Their fears. Their need to believe in something beyond the noise of everyday life.

Tom Elliott passed away on July 3, 2023. But before he did, he managed something rare: he built a space where belief and skepticism could coexist without tearing each other apart. A place where curiosity wasn't treated as a threat, but as something worth protecting.

That kind of philosophical breathing room—where emotional openness met intellectual honesty—shaped me more than any single investigation ever had. It was rewarding in its own right. But eventually, it wasn't enough. I found myself going through the motions, growing restless with chasing cold spots and reacting to flickering LEDs. I didn't want to keep playing along. I wanted a method, a framework grounded in engineering, critical thinking, and measurable evidence. I wanted rigor. Purpose. Something bigger than belief alone.

That's what drove me to form my own investigative team— one rooted in science, not spectacle. A team that didn't just follow claims, but studied the conditions that created them. Whether the trail led to ghosts or not. I was ready to ask harder questions. And I was no longer willing to settle for soft answers. I wanted to build something—something structured. Something real.

CHAPTER THREE

SIGNAL IN THE SILENCE

Breaking away to form my own team wasn't just a next step—it was a declaration. Use science to explore the unexplained. No theatrics. No blind acceptance. No chasing shadows because it felt good. I wasn't interested in preserving the mythology of the paranormal—I wanted to interrogate it. I wanted to understand how anomalies occurred, whether they could be replicated, and what—if anything—was actually happening beneath the surface of these experiences.

It wasn't enough to collect stories. I wanted data. Patterns. Something reproducible. I wanted to peel back the layers of assumption and superstition, and see what remained when all the noise was stripped away. To do that, I needed a new kind of team. So I put out the call.

By that point, I had built a modest but growing network—investigators, engineers, researchers—from teams scattered across the country. Geography didn't matter to me. Mindset did. I was looking for people who valued method over myth. People who were patient, analytical, and unafraid to say, "*I don't know*." Because that's where real investigation starts—not in certainty, but in doubt.

Para-Boston Meeting - Paul Piva, Mike Locke, Bart Smith, Michael Baker, Laura Giuliano, and Joe Rainone 2016

Most of the early members came from a group called Para-Boston—a spin-off of the larger Boston Paranormal team, founded by a guy named Scott Trainito. Para-Boston had formed for reasons that mirrored my own: tighter standards, more selective membership, a desire to do better. But as solid as they were, the group wasn't as focused on research or experimentation as I hoped to be. So it made sense to keep building—something new, something of our own.

The remaining members came from smaller, unrelated teams scattered across the Northeast. When it all came together, we called ourselves the New England Center for the Advancement of Paranormal Science—NECAPS, for you acronym nuts.

I'll admit, it was an impressive roster. We had a psychologist, a child therapist, biologists, and geologists. For the first time, it felt like we weren't just assembling a team—we were laying the foundation for a legitimate research group. You could feel the potential in the room. But potential didn't spare us from growing pains, we certainly had our share. Still, I was proud of what we'd built.

THE CORRELATION STUDY

We had brains we had motivation, and more than anything, we had ambition. Rather than diving headfirst into individual investigations, we decided to zoom out and ask a different question: *What if the answers weren't in any one haunting—but in the collective data across hundreds of them?*

Radical sure, but I wanted to explore broader correlations—patterns that might emerge when you look at paranormal reports not as isolated cases, but as pieces of a larger, environmental puzzle.

Could there be a connection between hauntings and the land itself? Were places built near underground rivers or quartz deposits more likely to generate reports of paranormal activity? And what about the invisible forces—electromagnetic fields, changes in barometric pressure, ultraviolet light, or solar radiation? Did those play a role?

I started to wonder if sightings of UFOs or cryptids—

creatures like Bigfoot—showed up in the same areas where ghost encounters were being reported. Was there overlap? And beyond the environmental side, what about the human factor? Were there psychological patterns among the people who reported these experiences? These were the kinds of questions that started to guide our work.

Twenty-three environmental and anomalous variables we thought were worth tracking were identified. If hauntings left any kind of measurable trace—an environmental fingerprint— we wanted to find it. Not to prove ghosts were real, but to look for patterns. And in science, patterns are where progress begins.

Our first step was to build a database—a catalog of allegedly haunted locations, as many as we could find. We cast the net wide, pulling from books, websites, historical archives, and personal accounts.

Once we had a workable list, we created a simple rating system for each site—ranking them based on the number of witnesses, the consistency of reports, and the overall quality of any supporting evidence.

From the outset we knew that the data would be shaky. Some of it was anecdotal. Some of it bordered on folklore. But none of that mattered—we weren't treating the reports as proof. We just needed a place to start. A trail to follow. Once the list was assembled, we turned to one of the era's most unexpectedly powerful tools: Google Earth—At the time, it felt like having private access to a satellite.

Each location was manually plotted on the map and their global coordinates were collected. From there, we began building overlays—called KML files—and layered different types of environmental data directly on top of our haunted site map. Geological data was pulled from the U.S. Geological Survey, fault lines were mapped, elevation and proximity to water sources was measured, and overlays for mineral deposits was added. Where available, we incorporated electromagnetic field readings and even solar activity records. And we didn't stop there.

We layered maps of cemeteries, railroad tracks, ley lines, and other stereotypically "*haunted*" sites and even imported clustering data from UFO sightings, Bigfoot reports, and other cryptid hotspots. If it had even the slightest whiff of the unexplained, we looked for a way to visualize it. What we ended up with was a sprawling, living spreadsheet of raw data—and a dense, multilayered virtual map packed with potential connections waiting to be tested. We were hunting patterns.

The value of this kind of research was straightforward: if we could uncover trends—correlations between environmental elements and reported paranormal activity— we might be able to identify where investigations were most likely to yield results. Just as importantly, we could rule out areas less likely to produce anything measurable. It was about working smarter. If we could spot patterns, we could stop chasing our tails and start testing with intention. As the data set grew and more comparisons were layered in, the first patterns to emerge weren't the ones we expected. In fact, the strongest early correlation had nothing to do with ghosts at all.

UFO sightings, as it turned out, consistently clustered near unusual geological features—fault lines, mineral-rich basins, and regions dense with granite or quartz. The more locations we mapped, the more that pattern held. Even stranger, Bigfoot sightings also tended to fall within just a few miles of those same UFO clusters. We hadn't gone looking for that connection—but there it was, undeniable on the screen. Not a slam dunk, but enough to take notice.

Ghost reports were harder to pin down. The correlations were subtler. We found a modest connection with natural water sources—especially rivers and lakes. That wasn't entirely surprising; folklore has linked spirits to water for centuries. But what did catch us off guard was a repeated association with railroad tracks. That one made the whole team pause. It wasn't something we'd anticipated, yet the data was consistent.

But the biggest surprise? Cemeteries. Or rather, the lack of them. Despite decades of horror movies, ghost tours, and Halloween clichés, there was no meaningful correlation between hauntings and cemeteries. None. For all their atmosphere and dramatic lighting, graveyards turned out to be among the least likely places to produce consistent paranormal reports. So if you've always assumed every cemetery is haunted—I've got numbers that say otherwise.

The correlation project continued quietly in the background, its spreadsheets and mapping tools steadily ticking forward, even as the team shifted focus to more hands-on investigations.

As valuable as the pattern-mapping work was, it was massive in scope. Slow. Labor-intensive, and not easily repeatable on a case-by-case basis. We needed something we could test now. If NECAPS. was going to succeed as a science-driven group, we had to identify a phenomenon that was both common and repeatable—something that appeared regularly at purportedly haunted locations and could be tested across multiple environments.

EVP HYPOTHESIS

The EM field-source issue was still unresolved. The audio direction finder was promising, but still in development. The geological correlation study was growing, but far from conclusive. What we needed was something tangible. Accessible. Testable. That "*something*" turned out to be EVP.

EVP came up constantly during the filming of *14 Degrees*. For most teams, it was the cornerstone. They'd sit in pitch-black rooms, ask questions into the silence, and later, comb through the recordings—hoping to catch whispers no one had heard in the moment. But the truth was, most of what passed for EVP wasn't paranormal at all.

More often than not, it was nothing more than environmental noise—static, low-frequency hums, the shuffle of a chair, the brush of a coat sleeve. And sometimes, it was even simpler than that. Pareidolia: A form of anthropomorphism—our tendency to assign human traits to non-human things. We're especially susceptible to it with sound. A faint rustle morphs into a whispered word. A breath reshapes itself into a name.

It's not deception—it's design. Our brains are built to find patterns, to make sense of the noise, even when there's nothing meaningful there. That's how we're wired. But even with all the rational, plausible explanations laid out… I had to admit—some of the recordings didn't fit. They resisted easy answers. And that's what kept me in the game.

Every so often, a recording would stop me cold. Clear. Distinct. Fully formed words or sentences, captured on gear that had been carefully monitored in spaces where no one had said a word. And not just in other people's footage—I'd caught a few of them myself. Moments where everything seemed normal in real time… until playback revealed something no one remembered hearing. That's when I began asking the one question I couldn't believe more people weren't asking: *How?*

How does a voice—one no one hears in the moment—end up on a recording? If these voices were real—if they weren't the result of contamination, interference, or imagination—then how were they getting there? What was the actual delivery mechanism?

This is where my background gave me an edge. I'd spent years as both an electronics engineer and a musician—two disciplines that rarely overlap, but in this case, came together perfectly. It gave me a unique lens through which to view the problem, not as a paranormal mystery, but as a question of physics and signal flow.

Because here's what we knew: EVPs had been captured on everything—reel-to-reel tape decks, cassette recorders, digital audio recorders, camcorders, even answering machines. That ruled out the format. It wasn't the tape. It wasn't the memory card. It wasn't the brand of equipment or the software. So what did all those devices have in common? A microphone.

No matter the era, no matter the model, every recording device shares the same basic input: a microphone. And for all our technological progress, the fundamentals of microphone design haven't changed much in the last century. At its core, a microphone does one thing: it converts sound into signal. It takes the vibration of air—caused by a voice, a breath, a footstep—and transforms it into a tiny electrical pulse that can be amplified, stored, and eventually played back.

In a standard dynamic microphone, this is done mechanically. Sound waves strike a thin diaphragm, causing it to vibrate. That diaphragm is attached to a coil of wire, suspended within a magnetic field provided by a ceramic magnet. As the coil moves with the sound, it generates a small electric current in the wire. No batteries. No software. Just motion, magnetism, and physics.

Condenser microphones work a little differently. Instead of using a coil and a magnet like dynamic mics, they rely on two very thin plates placed close together—one of which is a flexible diaphragm that moves when sound hits it.

As the diaphragm vibrates, the distance between the two plates changes. That movement alters something called capacitance—a material's ability to store electrical charge. When the distance shifts, so does the charge between the plates. That changing electrical signal becomes the sound we record.

Because of this design, condenser mics need an external power source—usually something called phantom power (i.e. *a battery*). But in return, they're far more sensitive. They can detect finer details, higher frequencies, and softer sounds—making them a favorite in recording studios.

Two different technologies. Two different approaches. But the same goal: air in, electricity out. That's the foundation of every audio recording.

So if an EVP wasn't just a trick of the brain—if it wasn't pareidolia or background noise—then something had to be interacting with the microphone at a deeper level. Not sound. Not vibration. But something else. Something invisible that could still influence the electrical components inside the mic. That was the mystery I wanted to explore.

What fascinated me most was this: microphones don't respond only to sound. The internal components—coils and capacitors—can also react, sometimes quite noticeably, to electromagnetic fields.

In dynamic microphones, the coil is designed to generate an electrical signal when it moves through a magnetic field. But here's the key: you don't always need movement. A nearby fluctuating electromagnetic field can induce a current in that coil through a process called *inductance*. In simple terms, inductance is when a changing magnetic field produces electricity in a wire—even if nothing is physically touching that wire. It's the same principal found in a wireless phone charger.

Capacitors, found in condenser microphones, are equally sensitive. They can be affected by nearby electrical energy, causing slight shifts in their stored charge—variations that can mimic real audio signals.

That's why you sometimes hear odd clicks, hums, or buzzes in recordings made near fluorescent lights, radios, or smartphones. It's not sound in the traditional sense—it's interference. Energy, not air pressure. If energy could leave a mark without making a sound... what else might be getting through?

That realization hit me like lightning. A Eureka moment. It

didn't mean ghosts were real. It didn't mean I'd discovered some paranormal smoking gun. But it did mean there was a plausible, mechanical explanation—a real-world, testable mechanism—for how voices might sometimes appear on recordings when nothing was audibly heard in the room. It gave me a foothold. For the first time since I'd started down this strange path, I felt like I wasn't just chasing shadows—I was starting to catch up to them. And not with folklore or blind faith, but with circuitry, physics, and signal theory. The idea itself was staggering.

Forget ghosts for a moment. Just the notion that a voice—or something like it—could exist as a purely electromagnetic imprint was enough to warrant real attention. Even without the supernatural angle, the idea had scientific weight. And before anyone jumps in with "radio interference," let me explain.

Yes—microphones, especially ones with poor shielding, can sometimes pick up stray radio signals. But here's the thing: radio waves don't carry sound the way your ears do. You don't just "*hear*" radio through the air. Instead, radio waves carry encoded information. Think of it like a secret message hidden inside a much faster wave—called a carrier. The real audio—voices or music—is tucked inside that carrier wave using a process called modulation. To hear that message, you need something that can decode it. That's what a radio receiver does—it strips away the carrier wave and recovers the original sound. That decoding process is called demodulation.

A regular microphone doesn't have any of that decoding ability. It can't demodulate a signal. So even if a microphone coil picks up part of a passing broadcast, it's not going to play a DJ's voice or a pop song. At most, you'll hear clicks, hums, or garbled noise. Which is why, when we recorded something that actually sounded like a human voice—with inflection, pacing, even emotion—it didn't make sense. It wasn't the local radio bleeding through. It was something different. And that's what raised the stakes.

So I set a goal: prove the idea. If there was even a chance that some kind of voice-like signal—carried not through sound waves in air, but through electromagnetic energy—could be picked up by a microphone coil, I wanted to recreate it. Under controlled conditions.

I pulled out my stash of spare parts—leftovers from my days repairing musical gear—and started sketching out ideas. This wasn't about catching a ghost. It was about building an experiment. A way to show that energy—pure, invisible energy—might leave a trace that sounded an awful lot like a voice. If I could pull it off—even once—then maybe those strange EVP recordings weren't so impossible after all.

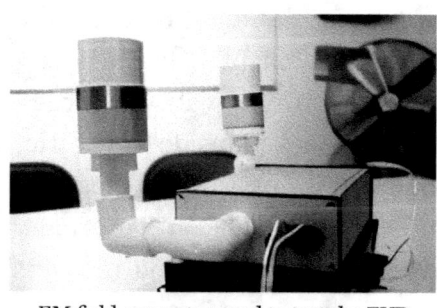

EM field generator used to test the EVP hypothesis. 2009

I started with something simple: a guitar pickup. These are small devices used in electric guitars to capture string vibrations using a magnetic field. I soldered it to a standard 1/8-inch plug—the kind that fits into the mic port of a handheld recorder. Then I picked up a pair of speaker coils. Normally, these are found inside speakers and used to move a cone that pushes air to create sound. But I wasn't attaching them to speaker cones. I didn't want sound. I wanted silence—at least to the ear.

The goal was to use those coils to silently broadcast a magnetic signal into the air. I wired them to a standard audio amplifier, loaded up some music, and started playing it through the coils. To any person standing in the room, it was completely silent—no speakers, no vibrations, nothing you could hear.

Then I placed the guitar pickup about six inches away from the coils and hit record. When I played the recording back? There it was. Music. Clear, full-fidelity audio—captured by the recorder, even though no one in the room had heard a thing. It was my first proof of concept. And I wasn't just smiling—I was beaming.

Next, I refined the test. I removed the guitar pickup and simply held a handheld recorder near the speaker coils. Same result. The music came through on playback—slightly quieter this time, but still present. Because the recorder's built-in mic was active, it also picked up ambient sound—footsteps, breathing, the rustle of movement—just like every EVP session I'd ever watched. And in that moment, it hit me: I had just replicated one of the most prized *"paranormal"* phenomena.

I had made a voice—well, music—appear on a recording. Unheard in the moment, crystal clear on playback. And I could do it on command. The test worked. Every time. Even more interesting: it didn't matter which microphone I used. Dynamic mics, lavaliers, handheld recorders—they all picked up the signal. But dynamic microphones consistently delivered a stronger, cleaner result, and that made sense.

Dynamic microphones work through electromagnetic induction, unlike their condenser counterparts. Their larger internal coils actually make them more receptive to certain kinds of electrical interference. But even so, neither type is meant to detect stray magnetic fields. That's not what they're built for. Still, better performance from the dynamic mic stuck with me, and posed a question. What if I removed sound from the equation entirely? No diaphragm. No air movement. Just the raw interaction between a magnetic field and a coil of wire. I wanted to strip it down to the essentials—to test whether a signal could be created without sound playing any role at all. So I got to work.

I built my own coils—hand-wound lengths of 22-gauge copper wire—the same type used in guitar pickups and microphone construction. I used PVC pipe for housing.

Some coils had magnet cores, like traditional dynamic microphones. Others were air coils, wound tightly to isolate electromagnetic sensitivity alone. I tested dozens of configurations: different wire densities, core materials, and shielding techniques.

My workspace looked like a mess of wires, hot glue, and scavenged components. But piece by piece, it started coming together, and what excited me most was this: I could now record for EVPs without worrying about human sound contamination. No coughs. No whispers. No footfalls. These coil mics weren't listening to sound—they were listening to something else entirely. Something quieter. Stranger. Maybe even impossible. All that remained was a real-world test. I had no idea what to expect.

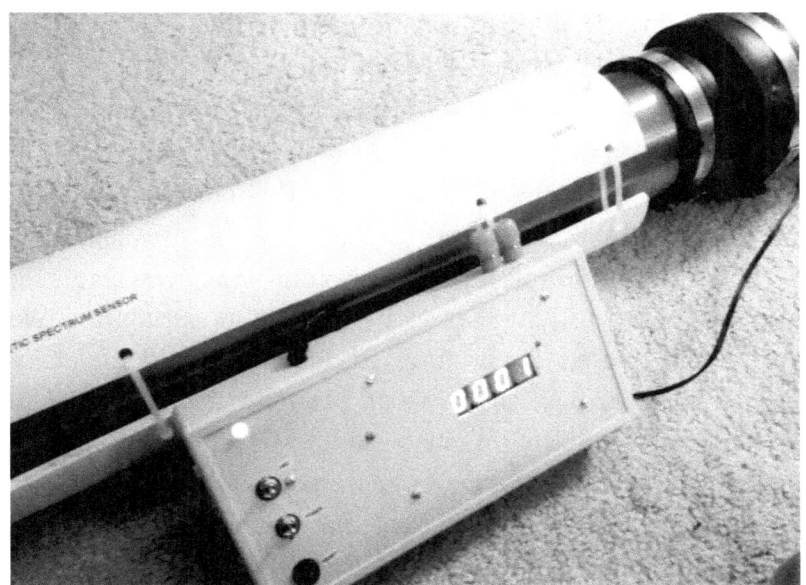

High sensitivity coil mic with event counter. This device would count spikes created by the coil so it could be left unattended. 2013.

THE MERGER

With the kind of equipment that might finally anchor the work in science—and a team that looked exactly like the one I had always imagined, smart and motivated and unwilling to drift into superstition—I believed, for once, that I was on the right path. It felt like the first time the dream and the reality lined up.

But there was a catch, one that theory had never managed to expose. Out in the field, it came down hard. Methodology, when spoken of in a quiet room, feels almost holy: orderly, reasoned, beyond reproach. In a landscape crowded with folklore and fueled by emotion and television dramatics, rigor was the one thing that promised credibility. And yet, in practice, the truth landed with an edge I hadn't anticipated. Science doesn't sell.

We weren't the team storming into homes with blinking gadgets and dramatic one-liners. We didn't swing EM field meters like lightsabers or shout into the void demanding a sign. We didn't promise to confirm your house was haunted. We didn't deal in jump scares or comforting certainties. We were there to test. To observe. To document. And for many homeowners, that wasn't what they wanted. They said they wanted answers. But often, what they really wanted was confirmation. Reassurance. A narrative that validated their experiences—not one that dissected them under a microscope. I couldn't blame them.

For the sincere, paranormal experiences are personal. Emotional. Sometimes even traumatic. And when people invited us into their homes, they weren't always looking for the truth. They were looking for meaning. And that made our approach—our objectivity—something of a liability.

We weren't struggling, but we weren't flooded with cases either. Other teams with flashier methods were booked solid. We, by contrast, saw fewer inquiries. It wasn't discouraging, exactly. But it was a reminder: truth-seeking isn't always the most marketable service. Still, we had allies. Several local teams respected our work and helped us gain access to promising locations. Often, we were called in after the fact— to follow up on unusual data or provide a second opinion. Over time, we developed a reputation. Not for spectacle—but for follow-through. That's when a bigger opportunity presented itself.

Para-Boston—one of the more established teams in the region—was exploring ways to introduce more scientific rigor into their investigations. Meanwhile, we were looking to expand our reach, to test our theories in new environments and with a broader audience. A merger made sense. They had visibility and trust. We had methodology and a hunger for data. So we joined forces. And just like that, the scope of our work grew. We had new tools, new locations, and a larger platform to explore our ideas.

Our first collaborative goal was simple: find a site where we could finally put the coil microphone to the test. I had already run a few trials at home. Nothing structured—just casual recordings during the day, letting the device run while I worked. The idea was to see how it performed in a controlled, familiar environment. After all, the device was built to eliminate traditional audio contamination. If anything unusual showed up, I could rule out all the usual culprits—no whispers, no shuffling feet, no environmental noise. What I got instead was something else entirely: a wall of interference. Unrelenting, ambient electromagnetic noise—Wi-Fi routers, Bluetooth devices, switching power supplies, kitchen appliances.

An invisible storm of signals bouncing through the air at all times. Not exactly the kind of mysterious anomaly I was hoping for—but it was a useful failure. And like most useful failures, it sparked another idea—one I'd come back to later.

For now, we needed a proper test. A real location. A place with history, credible witness reports, and just enough mystery to justify the experiment. We chose a site that had already earned our trust. Familiar territory. No theatrics, no headline-grabbing events—but a history of quiet, subtle anomalies that never quite added up. The Wayside Inn. Tucked away in Sudbury, Massachusetts, the Wayside Inn is more than just a historic landmark—it's a living artifact. One of the oldest operating inns in the United States, its legacy stretches back more than three centuries. It even inspired Henry Wadsworth Longfellow's Tales of a Wayside Inn. In short: if you were trying to cast a classic haunted location, this would be your set piece.

Over the years, guests and investigators alike reported strange activity throughout the property. But one room always stood out. Room 9. Once the private quarters of a woman named Jerusha Howe, Room 9 had become the epicenter of the inn's paranormal lore.

Visitors described disembodied whispers, phantom footsteps, and the faint strains of piano music drifting through the air when no one was around. Some claimed to wake with the feeling of being touched. Others saw shadows pass through the room despite being alone.

There were no flying chairs. No screaming specters. Just a persistent thread of quiet, consistent accounts—all centered on a single space. From a research perspective, that made Room 9 nearly perfect.

Our approach at the Wayside Inn was straightforward. We'd meet as a team in the early evening, unload equipment, and begin setup. After collecting baseline readings and running diagnostics, most of the team would head out. One or two volunteers would remain behind—either staying awake to monitor the room or sleeping in the space itself to document any changes through the night. It wasn't glamorous, but it was

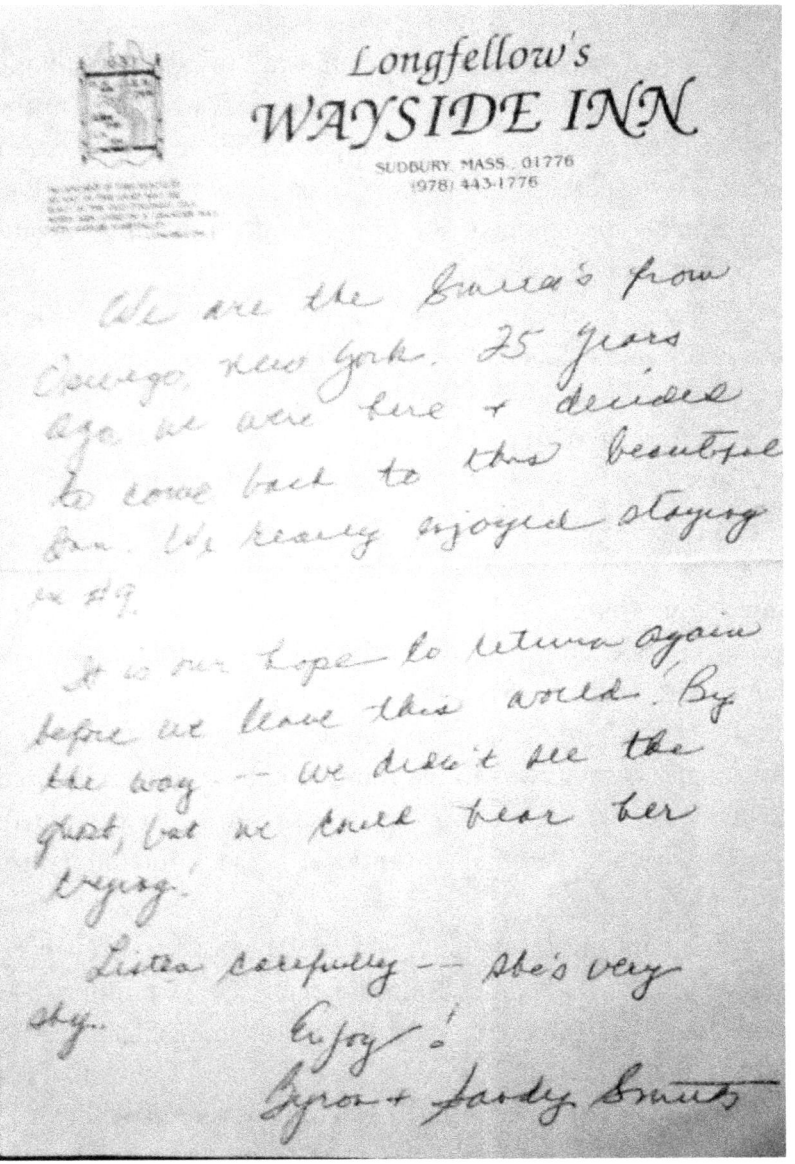

Letter written by former *Wayside Inn* guest describing crying in room 9.

functional.

For this experiment, we placed the coil microphone on the dresser near the bed in Room 9—right at head height, in the spot where many guests had reported feeling touched or hearing whispers. We didn't have hard data to justify that placement, only a hunch. But in this work, sometimes a well-reasoned hunch is all you get.

The next morning, we packed up the equipment and left. Back at home, I loaded the files and started combing through the audio. At first, it was exactly what I expected: five hours of silence, broken only by the occasional creak of floorboards or the rustle of a blanket shifting under someone's weight. Background noise. Nothing unusual.

I was just about to file it away as another null result—one more data point in a long list of maybes—when I switched gears and opened the file from the coil mic. Around the five-hour mark, I froze. Something had broken the silence. Not static. Not a hum. This wasn't an accidental whisper from a teammate. No one was in the room talking. No one muttered in their sleep. The microphone wasn't brushed or bumped. This wasn't audio in the conventional sense. Something else. A woman. Crying.

Not a faint sniffle or a quiet whimper, but a deep, wrenching sob—the kind that comes from the chest. Grief, unfiltered. It lasted less than fifteen seconds. But it was unmistakable. And it was undeniably human. The part I couldn't shake? That microphone wasn't designed to pick up any sound. And yet... there she was.

We had captured something that wasn't audible in real time—through a device that wasn't even designed to detect sound. And it wasn't radio interference, either. Radio waves don't carry continuous, unbroken clips of a woman crying. Not like this. And even if they did, what station plays fifteen seconds of raw, isolated sobbing at 1:30 in the morning? No music. No intro. No voiceover. No context.

It wasn't imagination. And it certainly wasn't nothing. It was something—something that didn't fit. And for the first time, we had real-world evidence that Electronic Voice Phenomena might not be just misheard noise or the power of suggestion. It might actually be electromagnetic in nature. That moment didn't give us all the answers. But it confirmed one thing: we were asking the right questions.

If it *was* a discovery—and I believe it was—it felt less like a breakthrough and more like a rupture. A tear in the boundary between assumption and possibility. The kind of moment that doesn't just add to the conversation—it forces you to rethink the premise entirely. And like all true discoveries, it brought more than excitement. It brought questions. The kind that follow you out of the field. The kind that don't let you sleep.

If EVP is electromagnetic in nature. Is that what's triggering the K-II meters? Are the EM field spikes we chase just side effects—fragments of signals we've never known how to receive? Are these voices we capture residual—some kind of imprint stored in the environment like data on a tape? Or are they live transmissions, generated in real time by something with intent? What allows them to break through? Is there a specific frequency? A threshold? A catalyst? Could we recreate it—on purpose?

The questions piled up faster than I could write them down. And even as they threatened to overwhelm me, one thing stayed clear: This wasn't a fluke. It wasn't just an anomaly buried in a hard drive or an unexplained glitch in the gear. It was a doorway. A starting point for something bigger. What I had—what we had—was more than just a strange recording. It was the first glimmer of a method. A tool. A systematic, repeatable process for approaching one of the most elusive aspects of paranormal research. And for the first time, the work felt grounded.

This wasn't about validating ghost stories or proving someone's childhood home was haunted. It was about uncovering something real—however small, however fragile—that could be tested, refined, and studied.

This was the edge of a new kind of research. And maybe, just maybe, the beginning of a new era for a field long driven by belief and speculation. Because belief without evidence was never enough for me. I wanted evidence. And now—for the first time—I had reason to believe it could be found.

CHAPTER FOUR

INVENTIONAL WISDOM

Discovery isn't a conclusion—it's a doorway. Once I considered the possibility that EVP might travel through electromagnetic pathways, I found myself consumed by a single question: how do you truly listen? Not just hear, but listen—cleaner, louder, with sharper resolution. And just as important, how do you analyze what you've captured? That's when I discovered spectrogram analysis.

In the paranormal world, audio is traditionally reviewed using waveform analysis. Picture a jagged line moving across a screen, rising and falling with the volume. You can tell when a sound occurred, but not what it was. A word? A breath? The moan of a radiator? You're left guessing. It's one-dimensional—useful, but incomplete.

A waveform is like viewing a photo of a skyline: tall buildings, sharp shadows—but no sense of how it all fits together. But step back—way back—and the view changes. Imagine a satellite image of the entire city. You see the grid: streets, traffic patterns, parks, neighborhoods. A layout. A map.

That's what a spectrogram offers—a fuller view of sound. Instead of tracking only amplitude over time, a spectrogram shows frequency, intensity, and duration. Every sound— whether human speech or ambient noise—has a unique fingerprint. In a spectrogram, those fingerprints become visible. You don't just hear a whisper or a knock. You see its shape. To me, that was a personal breakthrough.

Suddenly, I wasn't just listening to sound—I was reading it. I threw myself into the mechanics of speech. I learned to spot plosives—those sharp bursts of air in sounds like p and t. I studied fricatives—like f and s—where air flows through a narrow space, creating a hiss. I learned the difference between voiced and unvoiced consonants, and how vowel transitions shape the rhythm of speech. These weren't abstract linguistic terms anymore—they were patterns I could see and recognize instantly.

I trained my eyes to spot phonemes—the building blocks of words—the same way someone might scan a crowd and recognize a familiar face. Eventually, I could look at a spectrogram—a visual graph of sound over time—and recognize speech before I ever hit play.

Word spread, slowly but steadily. People started reaching out. Friends of friends. Investigation teams who'd heard I could *make sense of the noise.* But I wasn't guessing. I wasn't trusting instinct or interpretation. I was reading the visual signature of sound.

I didn't chase a spotlight. I didn't take the stage at big conferences. But I found places to share what I knew—libraries, community centers, anywhere with a blank wall to project on.

Sometimes five people showed up. Sometimes just two. But the ones who stayed? They were riveted. Once you see speech—really see it—it changes everything. I'd walk them through a sentence without audio. Just visuals. And like magic, they'd follow the words. Not because I was guessing. Because speech has a shape. Plosives land like bricks. Vowels rise and fall in arches. Fricatives drift like fog. You start trusting your eyes more than your ears. And when I paired this knowledge with a device I'd built—a coil microphone that ignored traditional sound—I knew I had something. Every recording became an EM field excavation. No longer '*listening*' for voices. I was scanning for structure—looking for the geometry of communication embedded in the static. And sometimes, I found it. But it wasn't just speech that surfaced.

THE NOISE BETWEEN THE LINES

Other patterns began to emerge—frequencies that didn't behave like language. Harmonics that lingered too long. Mechanical hums, low and steady. hovering just below the threshold of human hearing.

They weren't voices. But they weren't random either. They repeated across recordings, in different places, at different times. Always with a shape. Always with structure. That's when I understood: I hadn't just built a microphone. I'd built a window. Not to the other side—but to a part of this world we rarely notice. The electromagnetic terrain that surrounds us.

Every signal that once sent ghost-hunting gadgets into a frenzy—those blinking lights, those chirping meters—was now laid bare. Unmasked. Quantified. Sixty-hertz hum? Power lines. Rhythmic pulses? Refrigerators. Staccato bursts? Cell phones checking for towers. Each signal, once mistaken for a whisper from beyond, revealed itself as a product of the modern world—mundane, mechanical, but traceable.

I was mapping noise, and yet, even in the clarity, I couldn't stop. Because somewhere in that signal-rich wilderness, something occasionally flickered that didn't belong. A glitch in the pattern. An outlier that behaved too deliberately to ignore. So I went back to the bench.

If the coil mic could reveal something hidden—something we couldn't hear in real time—I wanted to push it further. Refine it. Sharpen it. So I started building variations. Dozens of them.

I tested different types of wire, from hair-thin 30-gauge strands to thick, sturdy 12-gauge coils. I swapped out air cores for ferrite—a dense, magnetic material often used to boost signal response. I built frames from whatever I had on hand: PVC pipe, hollowed-out blocks of wood, even old radio casings I pulled from the scrap pile. Some coils had magnets. Others didn't. I wasn't aiming for pretty. I was aiming for sensitivity.

I felt like I was swimming through a sea of copper wire and breadboards, clipped leads curling like ivy across my desk. I scribbled notes in the margins of old notebooks, soldered in the quiet hours, and fell asleep with the tang of flux still on my hands.

Most builds failed. That was expected. Some overloaded instantly. Others picked up so much environmental junk they became unusable. But now and then, something worked—just enough to keep going. A shift in clarity. A sharper signal. A pattern in the chaos. And along the way, I found something even more critical than coil design: orientation.

Electromagnetic fields don't radiate like light. They move along vectors—directional lines that determine what's sensed and what's missed. And so are the coils that detect them. Every sensor has an axis of sensitivity, an invisible line that determines what it hears and what it ignores. If your sensor isn't aligned with the source, you'll miss it—completely. I'd built sensitive gear. But I was pointing in the dark.

So I started testing. I'd place a coil in a room and rotate it by hand—degree by painful degree—logging the signal strength and scanning the spectrogram for shifts. It worked, technically, but it was slow. Inaccurate. Human. I needed precision. I needed consistency. I needed a way to let the data speak without my hands in the mix. So I built a robot.

A MACHINE FOR PATIENCE

The robot wasn't graceful. A tangle of servos, wires, and gears mounted on a piece of acrylic I'd scored and cut by hand in my basement. But it worked. It could rotate a coil through more than 300 unique angles, pausing at each one to capture and log signal strength. Every degree was a data point. Every spike, a clue. When a reading crossed a preset threshold, the machine flagged it, archived it, and stored the accompanying audio in a separate folder for review. At the heart of the rig was a six-inch cylindrical coil—22-gauge wire wound tightly around a ferrite core—with a condenser mic on each end. It recorded not just electromagnetic data, but also environmental conditions like temperature, humidity, and barometric pressure.

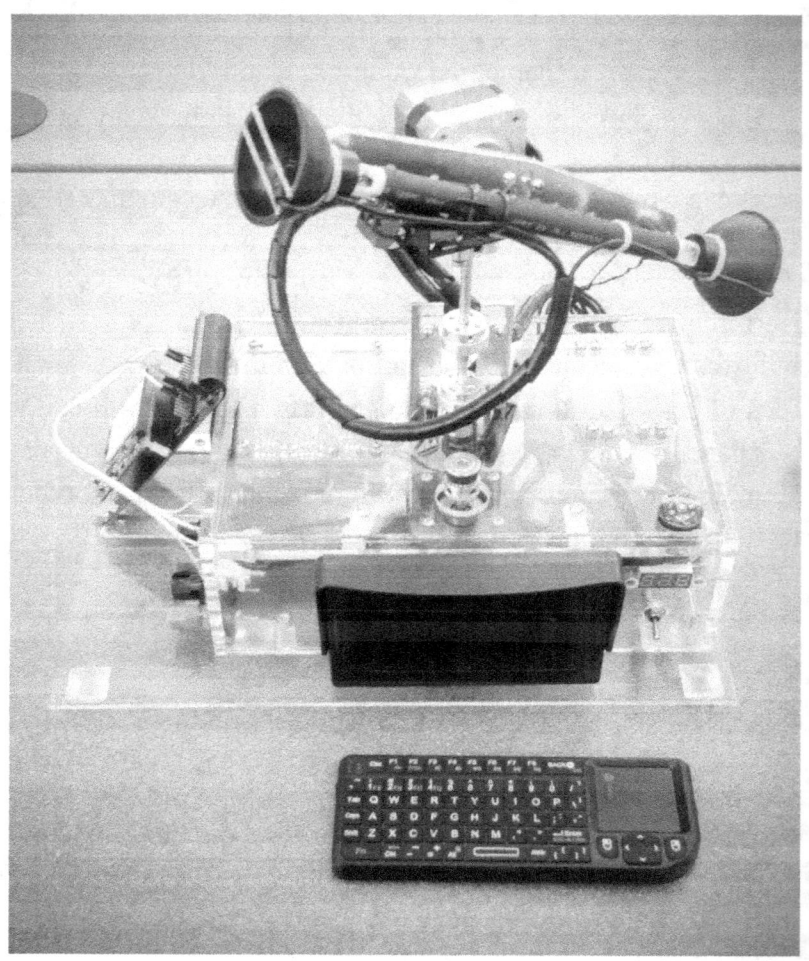

EM axis detection robot prototype with environmental measurement analysis.
Built in 2015.

I had no concrete reason to collect those additional metrics. But I've always believed that data is cheap, and you never know which thread might connect to another. Sometimes a correlation appears only after you've given it room to form.

Was it overkill? Maybe. But I needed uniformity. Repeatability. A way to cut through noise—both literal and figurative. I let the robot run for hours, days, sometimes weeks. Most of what it logged was ordinary—appliances cycling on, routers pinging the ether, microwaves singing their invisible song. But three recordings stood out. They weren't just spikes. They were structured. Patterned. Intentional. Each came from a different location, at a different time, and—most notably—each one peaked at a different axis. That detail stuck with me. If these were genuine anomalies, directionality mattered. But three samples don't make a pattern. They make a possibility. And possibility, in this work, is oxygen.

With the robot humming in the background, I shifted focus. There were other paths I hadn't fully explored—corners of physics I'd brushed up against but never really dug into.

EDDY CURRENTS

That's when I circled back to something I first saw in a high school science demo: eddy currents. Most people remember them from the magnet-and-copper-pipe trick. You drop a strong magnet into a metal tube, and instead of falling straight through, it slows down—gliding as if it's moving through molasses.

What's happening is surprisingly elegant. As the magnet

drops, its motion generates swirling electric currents inside the metal. Those little loops of current—called eddy currents—create their own magnetic fields, which push back against the falling magnet. The result? A slow, graceful descent. But what caught my attention wasn't the slowing—it was the swirling. Those tiny loops of energy. Because here's the thing: eddy currents don't always need movement. They can form even when nothing's physically shifting—as long as there's a changing magnetic field.

That got me thinking: what if some of the anomalies I'd been chasing weren't voices or signals, but interactions? Two fields intersecting. Not communication, but collision. And maybe—if we were lucky—a reaction. I wondered: could something intelligent—if such a thing existed—be disturbing electromagnetic fields in subtle, measurable ways? Could we detect that disturbance not as a message, but as a fingerprint left behind?

So I built a new kind of device. Not a recorder. Not a sensor. A watcher. A circuit designed to log evidence of interaction—those fleeting swirls of energy that don't belong. The concept was adapted from a proximity alarm—those discreet devices used in galleries and museums to alert staff when someone gets too close to a display.

A simple circuit emits a low-frequency electromagnetic field, and when another field—like the subtle electric aura of a human body—enters its space, the interaction causes a measurable voltage shift. Usually, it triggers a buzzer. But I didn't want a buzzer. I wanted a record. So I rewired the circuit. Instead of sounding an alarm, the system routed its output to a data logger. I added a seven-segment LED display—not to dazzle or dramatize, just to offer a live readout of the voltage fluctuations. A quiet, visual whisper.

The device would sit in a room, generate its own electromagnetic field, and wait. At its center, a single probe wire was clipped to

Eddy current monitor prototype. 2014

a nearby piece of metal—anything conductive: a pipe, a radiator, a filing cabinet. That object became the target, the canvas. If another field passed through—if there was interference, overlap, interaction—it might induce a trace of current in the metal. Not enough to shock, not enough to feel. But enough to log.

That was the moment I was after. The ripple. The echo of presence—not in the form of a voice or shadow, but in the subtle physics of convergence. And when it happened, the machine would catch it. No lights. No buzzers. Just a number. Logged. Time-stamped. Ready for analysis.

The device wasn't much to look at. Just a small plastic housing, some exposed wiring, a few hand-soldered joints, and the faint hum of potential. But it was something new—at least in this field. A way to test for interaction without anthropomorphizing the unknown. No leading questions. No haunted narratives. Just: *did something pass through*? What I was doing, essentially, was trying to make the invisible visible—not through belief or suggestion, but through measurement. I didn't know what I was looking for. But I knew what I didn't want: *ambiguity*. And that meant embracing the idea that a "*paranormal event*" might not look like anything we expect. It might not be a whisper or a face in the dark. It might be a deviation in field strength. A surge in induced current. A nudge so slight, it would only register if you were paying attention—and had the right tools to notice.

What surprised me most was how few others were looking in this direction. Ghost hunting had become saturated with gadgets that blinked and chirped, each one promising more than it delivered. But few asked what those devices were actually measuring. Fewer still questioned why. That's where I kept returning—not just to the tools, but to the principles behind them.

If we were going to claim science, we had to mean it. And that meant leaving behind the thrill of the unknown, and learning to sit, instead, with the precision of what could be known. Even if the answer was nothing.

THE VALUE OF STILLNESS

I kept the eddy current sensor running for months. I even built a couple more that I sold to a few colleagues. Not because I expected fireworks, but because I believed in the long arc of observation.

It wasn't the sort of device that rewarded impatience. Most nights, it sat in silence—logging numbers that rarely moved, tracking baseline levels that became so familiar I could spot a voltage drift with a glance. But occasionally, something shifted.

Once, while recording in an empty historical home, the

voltage spiked three times over a four-minute period—each time registering a subtle but measurable surge in the probe wire. There were no appliances nearby. No visible motion. No wireless devices in the room. And yet the readings were clean, unmistakable. Not dramatic. Just… different.

I've never claimed those spikes were paranormal. In fact, my first instinct was always to explain them—to check for hidden wiring, HVAC cycling, metal fatigue, anything that could account for the anomaly. And sometimes I found explanations. But not always, and those were the moments that kept me coming back. Not because they proved something, but because they didn't. They invited questions. They refused to settle into easy categories. And as frustrating as that was, it also felt honest.

In a field that so often leapt to conclusions, I found comfort in the pause. In the restraint. In the quiet act of noticing something strange and choosing not to name it too soon. That became the rhythm of my research: build, test, observe, question. Start again. I began to see every tool I built not just as a sensor, but as a translator—an interface between the world we understand and the one we only think we do.

Some devices clarified things. Others muddied the waters. But each one helped me refine my questions. And that, more than anything, was the real achievement: learning how to ask better questions.

LOST IN THE SHADOWS

Most of the tools I'd built up to that point were designed to detect energy that couldn't be seen—audio, electromagnetic fields, eddy currents. Invisible, abstract forces. Whether or not they meant anything was up for debate, but at the very least, they weren't part of the visible world. Still, there was one visual phenomenon that came up so often, I couldn't ignore it: moving shadows.

They were second only to EVP claims in terms of sheer volume. Practically every location I investigated had at least one story involving unexplained movement—usually dark, usually fast, usually just on the edge of perception. I'd even seen a few myself over the years.

What struck me most wasn't just the consistency of these claims, but one detail that kept surfacing: people said the shadows moved through open space, not along walls. They weren't just darker spots in a dim corner—they seemed to occupy space.

They seemed to have mass. And that's where my mind went: if something truly has mass—or at least density sufficient to block light—then it should be measurable. Detectable. There had to be a way to test that. So I set out to build a device that could detect even the faintest change in light levels—something sensitive enough to register a subtle shift in illumination and designed to detect tiny changes in light levels—specifically, shifts in brightness, the kind of minute change you'd miss with the naked eye.

At the heart of the system was a high-sensitivity light sensor—a component called the OPT101P, made by Texas Instruments. I mounted the sensor inside a narrow tube to block out any side light and aimed it at a flat white surface that was evenly lit by a steady light source. The idea was simple: if

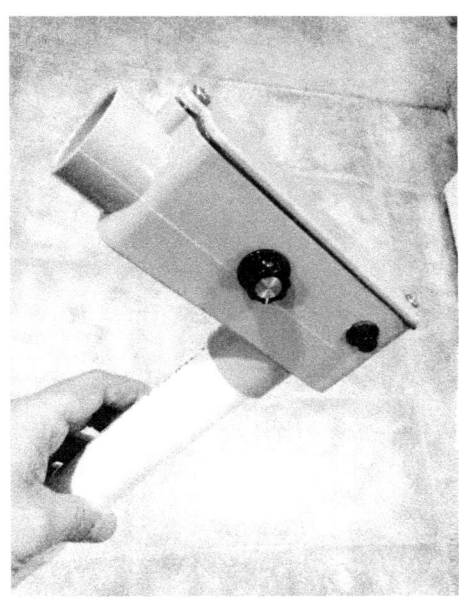

Shadow detector prototype. 2016

anything moved between the sensor and the reflector—something that could cast even the faintest shadow—the amount of light hitting the sensor would drop slightly. That drop in voltage could be measured and recorded.

The build itself was pretty straightforward. I used standard electrical conduit to house the sensor and mounted it on a tripod to keep it steady. To test it, I used thin trails of incense smoke and let them drift slowly through the detection path. Even the faintest wisp— barely visible—was enough to cause a measurable dip in the signal. It worked better than I expected.

The only real challenge was placement. The sensor wasn't going to stumble across shadows at random—it needed to be positioned somewhere with a history of reported activity. Ideally, a room where shadow movement had been consistently observed. Fortunately, we had one, and once again we returned to Room 9 at the Wayside Inn in Sudbury, Massachusetts.

Just a few months earlier, one of the Boston Paranormal team members, John Smith had rented the room alone to run a solo investigation. He didn't have much gear with him—just a

10/13/13

Had a lovely wedding here for our
daughter! Stayed in Room 10 — definitely
heard doors creaking in the middle of
the night. Our relatives were staying
in room 9 and spotted a shadow that
they could not explain. Great fun!!

Bob & Jan

One of many letters from a former *Wayside Inn* guest
describing a shadow on room 9.

camera, set to record through the night. At one point in the footage, two faint shadows could be seen rising from the floor and drifting across the bed as he slept. It was subtle, but unmistakable. We didn't know if it was a trick of the light, a glitch in the camera, or something environmental. But whatever it was, that room had earned a second look. The only problem was, every return visit cost nearly $150. It was still an inn, after all—and inns are in the business of making money. Fortunately, there were a few times I managed to barter for a night in the room.

One of those trades came in the form of a special event we pitched: An Evening with Jerusha. Jerusha was said to be the spirit that haunted Room 9. The plan was that I'd host a dinner at the inn, guiding guests through its full history, from its earliest days to the many changes it had seen over the years. The evening would culminate in a tour of Room 9—Jerusha's infamous bedroom—followed by a presentation of the footage and audio we had captured. I showed how the evidence we collected lined up with claims made by past guests—strange sounds, fleeting shadows, unexplained movement. All of this while guests dined on a period-authentic menu: chicken fricassee with spring vegetables.

The night was a success. And best of all, it earned a free room rental for the team—and a perfect chance to test out my new device.

On the night of the investigation, I directed the shadow detector in the exact spot where the movement had been caught on video months earlier.

In truth, I was hoping for a repeat performance. There wasn't much else to go on. Trying to determine *where* in a

room an anomaly might appear—assuming it appears at all—
is a guessing game at best. All I had was history. And in this
case, history was oddly consistent.

Michael Baker during shadow detector test at *Wayside Inn*. 2016

That same location had been mentioned in earlier reports
from other guests—accounts that predated the video entirely.
People described seeing shadows move across the room, often
tracing the same path: near the foot of the bed, slightly off-
center, just a few feet from where the camera had recorded that
odd upward sweep. It wasn't proof, but if you're looking for a
place to aim a sensor, recurring reports are as good a lead as
any.

Over the course of the evening, the readout on the detector
stayed mostly steady. A few minor dips occurred, but nothing
dramatic—just subtle changes that could've been caused by
anything from a minor voltage fluctuation in the power source

to a slight shift in the rig from someone walking across the room. None of our cameras caught anything out of the ordinary.

This is where the real challenge begins—not just technically, but statistically. Even if we set aside the possibility that shadow phenomena might not exist at all, the simple question of where and when to place a device is almost impossible to solve.

Most sensors—no matter how sensitive—can only monitor a limited area. They're like flashlights in a forest. If something happens just outside that beam, you'll miss it. It's not a flaw in the technology—it's a function of physical space. Unless you can blanket an entire room with detectors, you're always making an educated guess. And even the best guesses miss.

That night, nothing revealed itself. But that doesn't mean the idea behind the detector was flawed. It just confirmed what I already knew: this kind of research takes time. A lot of time. And patience. And, realistically, a decent amount of money— because waiting for lightning to strike sometimes means renting the same room over and over again, just to watch it not happen.

INFRA-SOUND

Beyond visual anomalies, there was another category of claims I wanted to address—those involving physical interaction. Not objects moving, necessarily, but more subtle forms of disturbance: *seismic activity and infra-sound*. It might sound extreme at first, but capturing seismic activity has real potential. If someone claims to hear unexplained

Infrasound detector prototype. 2016

footsteps, and you have a sensor capable of recording low-frequency vibrations in the floor—paired with time-stamped video confirming no one was present—you have a starting point for analysis.

Of course, that only works if the environment itself isn't interfering. Pipes, for example, can produce similar percussive signatures, especially when expanding or contracting. So placement matters. And so does context.

Infra-sound, on the other hand, is a different kind of invisible. It refers to low-frequency sound waves—typically below 20 Hz—that fall beneath the range of human hearing. At sufficient amplitude, infra-sound has been linked to a variety of physical and emotional responses: unease, sorrow, nausea, and the classic *"presence in the room"* sensation. It's not mystical. It's just physics interacting with biology. And it's precisely the kind of variable that could skew perception during an investigation.

Infra-sound can be generated naturally—by thunderstorms, wind patterns, waterfalls, or certain architectural structures that create low-frequency resonance. But regardless of the source, its potential influence on witnesses made it something I wanted to track. Which led to a device that could monitor both seismic activity and infra-sound at the same time.

The design was simple enough, but effective. I started with a six-inch PVC pipe and stretched a large balloon tightly over one end, clamping it in place. To the center of that balloon, I attached two neodymium (*rare earth*) magnets—one on each side of the membrane—suspended in the middle of the pipe's opening. I then mounted a coil microphone on a custom PVC arm, carefully positioning it just above the magnets without allowing contact. The spacing was critical: close enough to detect motion, far enough to avoid magnetic pull. From there, the coil mic was connected to my trusty voltage data logger. When the device sat on the floor, any low-level vibration— whether from footsteps, knocks, or distant movement—would cause the suspended magnets to shift slightly. That movement would induce a current in the coil mic, which the logger would record as a voltage change. During initial tests, I could register my own footsteps from more than twelve feet away.

The same system also worked for infrasound. Because infrasound moves air like any other soundwave—just at lower frequencies and often higher volumes—it caused the balloon to flex. That motion, however slight, was enough to shift the magnets and trigger the sensor. The balloon effectively acted as a diaphragm, turning invisible pressure changes into measurable data.

To test the setup, I simulated low-frequency air movement in two ways. First, I slammed a door in a sealed room. The pulse of air that followed registered on the logger. Then, I struck the side of a five-gallon water jug in a steady rhythm— producing a thudding bass note deep enough to simulate natural infra-sound. That worked too. The sensor picked it up.

With that, I had a tool that could track two important environmental variables. I built four of them and deployed them on as many investigations as I could. They proved useful—not in revealing anything anomalous, but in helping map the movement of my team and rule out human-generated interference.

As for unexplained footsteps or measurable infra-sound? Nothing ever surfaced. But to be fair I never heard unexplained footsteps or had any feelings of unease in the places I tested the gear. Maybe it was just bad timing. The absence of data doesn't mean the idea was flawed. It just meant I had built a better tool for understanding the environment—and sometimes, that's the only step forward you get.

Discovery isn't a single moment. It's a process. Slow. Often tedious. A steady accumulation of observations, missteps, adjustments—and every so often, a flicker of something unfamiliar. It's rarely dramatic. Most of the time, it isn't even satisfying. But it's real. And for me, that was enough.

The tools I built, the data I recorded, the hours spent hunched over spectrograms and voltmeters—it didn't lead to some grand breakthrough. I didn't prove a theory or uncover a secret. But it changed how I see the world. It sharpened my sense of what's possible. What if the real work isn't chasing answers—but learning to listen well enough to notice the question?

CHAPTER FIVE

EXPERIENCE BY DESIGN

If I'm going to be honest about my time in this field—what pulled me in, and ultimately, what pushed me out—then I have to talk about the gear. Not just the devices themselves, but the mindset that built them. Because if there's one thing quietly eroding the credibility of modern ghost hunting, it's the tools investigators have come to depend on—and the influence television has had in shaping how they're used.

Before I get too far, there's a small but important clarification I need to make. Throughout this book, I've referred to electromagnetic fields as EM fields. Some readers—particularly those familiar with today's paranormal investigation scene—might wonder why I don't just say "*EMF*," like everyone else.

Here's why: in physics, EMF doesn't stand for electromagnetic field. It stands for electromotive force—the voltage that drives electric current through a circuit. Somewhere along the way—starting in the late 1980s—manufacturers began marketing consumer-grade meters to ghost hunters, and the term EMF got misused. It stuck. So my choice to use EM fields isn't just semantics. It's a quiet attempt to steer things back toward accuracy. Now—back to the gear.

At first glance, it all looks impressive. Blinking lights. Rising tones. Sudden alarms. But look closer, and the logic starts to unravel. These tools weren't built on proven principles or refined through scientific testing. They were built around one thing: mystery. And mystery, in this world, is often mistaken for meaning.

If a light flashes in response to something we can't see—if a meter spikes from a force we don't understand—it's treated as evidence. Not because we know what caused it, but because we don't. That's the backwards logic at play: the less we understand a device's function, the more valuable it seems. Especially if it reacts to something invisible—like EM fields or stray radio signals.

To the average observer, that ambiguity becomes part of the appeal. *"If we don't know why it's going off,"* they say, *"maybe it's a ghost."* But real science doesn't work that way. You don't chase the unknown with tools you don't understand. You don't record unexplained results with unexplained devices and call it data. That's not investigation. That's performance. And in far too many cases, that's what paranormal research has become: a stage show, complete with props that look technical but tell us very little and investigators who understand very little about design and reasoning behind the equipment they use.

I could go on for days cataloging the insidious array of devices used in the field today. But ¯ won't. Not because they don't deserve scrutiny—they sure do—but because the problem isn't just the volume. It's the influence.

Some tools have become so embedded in ghost hunting culture that to question them feels almost sacrilegious. They've shown up in too many episodes, too many YouTube thumbnails, too many overnight live streams for anyone to openly accept the concept of them being, well, garbage.

So instead of dragging you through a laundry list of blinking, chirping distractions, I want to focus on just a few. The ones that didn't just fail to move the field forward—They pulled it in the wrong direction.

You've already met the K-II meter back in Chapter 2, where I described modifying it to log voltage instead of flashing lights. By then, I'd already seen its shortcomings up close—useful as a safety tool, but flimsy as science. Still, the K-II deserves another mention here, not for its engineering, but for what it represents.

The K-II didn't become a staple of paranormal research because it was precise. It became popular because it was dramatic. Early message boards buzzed with stories of its spikes, and by the late 2000s, television had turned it into a star. Psychic Chris Fleming featured it on *Psychic Kids*. *Ghost Hunters* waved it around like a hotline to the beyond. A row of LEDs climbing from green to red was visual shorthand for "*something's here.*" Viewers didn't need to know how it worked. They just needed to see it respond.

But what the K-II never offered—what it still can't offer—is context. It doesn't distinguish between a cell phone connection, a passing taxi, or a genuine anomaly. It reacts, blindly, to whatever electromagnetic field happens to cross its path. And yet in countless investigations, that reaction is treated as evidence.

That's the larger problem. In ghost hunting, ambiguity often carries more weight than certainty. A device that offers no explanation is often more appealing than one that does, because it leaves room for belief. The K-II is the perfect example of that logic: it thrives not because it delivers answers, but because it keeps the questions alive.

Blinking lights make for good television. They suggest momentum, mystery, the presence of the unseen. But science doesn't work on suggestion. And a tool that can only say *"something happened"* without telling you what, where, or why, isn't evidence. It's theater.

THE OVILUS

If the K-II is the mascot of ghost hunting, the Ovilus is its oracle. Since its debut in the mid-2000s, the device has gone through multiple versions—each one promising better accuracy, more features, and a stronger link to the beyond. But despite the cosmetic upgrades and added bells and whistles, the core premise has never really changed.

The Ovilus is marketed as a "spirit-communication" tool –"*for entertainment only*", don't forget that. A device that allows spirits to speak by manipulating environmental energy—specifically electromagnetic fields, temperature, or atmospheric changes—to trigger words from a pre-loaded digital dictionary. That's the idea, anyway.

According to its creator, the Ovilus is built around a combination of sensors, including EM field detectors, thermometers, and, in some versions, barometric or static field sensors. The claim is that these subtle environmental changes are interpreted by a proprietary algorithm and then mapped to specific words from a database—essentially translating ghostly intent into human language.

Believe it or not, there are also claims that it actually "*teaches*" ghosts how to respond. On paper, it sounds futuristic. Almost scientific. But when you step back and really consider it, the problems begin stacking up fast.

For one, the connection between environmental fluctuation and linguistic output is never clearly explained. What exactly determines which word gets chosen? Why that word, and not another? Is there a measurable correlation between the input and the response? The answer, more often than not, is a shrug. And that's where I come in.

Back in 2009, a close friend and longtime investigative partner—let's call her Kathy—approached me with a proposition. She had purchased an Ovilus herself, curious but skeptical. And after watching it spout eerie-sounding words at convenient moments, she wanted to know: was this thing actually reacting to anything? Or was it just... random?

She mailed the device to me and asked if I could dissect it. Physically, digitally, behaviorally. Run tests. Pull it apart. See if anything beneath the surface justified the claims. What I found was telling.

The device Kathy sent me was an Ovilus I—the original model. The first of its kind. Before I even opened it up, I wanted to see how it behaved under normal conditions. If it truly responded to environmental factors like EM field or temperature shifts. I powered it on and let it run. After a minute or so, it began to speak—slowly, in a thick, mechanical voice. Single words, spaced out at irregular intervals.

> *"Garden."*
> *"Red."*
> *"Window."*

None of them made sense. They weren't related to each other. They didn't match the environment I was in. And they certainly didn't tie into any personal history or alleged spirit presence. Just arbitrary nouns and adjectives.

I let the device run for about 20 minutes. In that time, it produced 18 words. No context. No response to stimulus. Just an eerie voice saying disconnected things into the room. Next, I wanted to put the sensors to the test.

If the device really used EM field and temperature data to trigger specific words, then exposing it to controlled environmental changes should produce measurable results. First up: electromagnetic fields.

To ensure it was exposed to a strong and variable EM signal, I brought in several high-output electrical devices— things that I knew from prior testing created significant electromagnetic interference. The first was a power drill. Not a battery-powered one—this was a heavy-duty corded model, the kind that sends EM field readings off the charts when running.

I powered it on within inches of the Ovilus and watched. Nothing. Not a single word. I moved the drill closer. Cycled it on and off. Switched outlets. Still nothing. The Ovilus remained silent. Then, a few minutes later, with the drill unplugged and sitting idle on the floor, it spoke.

"Mirror."

No EM field. No interaction. No Mirror. No known variable had changed. It became clear, very quickly, that the Ovilus wasn't reacting to electromagnetic fields at all. At least not in any way that was predictable or repeatable. And if it wasn't responding to EM field, then what was it doing?

Next, I wanted to test the Ovilus' temperature sensors so I put it in the most logical place I could think of to do just that—the freezer. Surely the temperature drop would prompt it to speak, right? *Wrong.*

Not a word for three full minutes—which, in sensor response time, is an eternity. And when it did speak, the words were sparse and nonsensical and then suddenly, while still in the freezer, the device went silent.

Now for the overload. I taped the trigger of my electric power drill to keep it spinning and I tossed it into the freezer with the Ovilus. Not a peep for almost 5 minutes! It was clear to me that this device did not work as it was claimed. Now was the time to crack it open.

When I removed the cover, I found a printed circuit board with several ICs—computer chips—and the usual supporting components: resistors, capacitors, and an operational amplifier for audio volume. The main chips appeared to be a text-to-speech processor and a large microcontroller, which presumably stored the word list fed into the speech engine.

What stood out wasn't what I found, but what I didn't. There was no Hall effect sensor, no induction coil, and no temperature probes—none of the components typically required to detect electromagnetic or thermal changes. What I did find was a single, open-ended wire soldered to one of the microcontroller's input pins.

It appeared to function as a makeshift antenna—essentially a noise trigger. When that wire picked up enough ambient electrical interference or static, it closed the digital switch in the IC and activated the speech system.

In other words, this wasn't detecting ghosts. It was detecting anything—random electrical noise, static charges, or even stray voltage surges. And once triggered, it simply read a random word from memory and spoke it aloud.

To demonstrate the randomness of the Ovilus, I decided to build a software version of it. Back in the early days, the manufacturer had posted a complete list of the words used by the Ovilus I on their website. Fortunately, I had saved a copy to my archives.

That was the list I used to create my digital replica. My version didn't include any sensors. It didn't scan the environment, detect changes in EM field, or monitor temperature. It simply pulled from the exact same vocabulary, in the exact same order as the original device, using a basic random number generator to select and speak words at a pace that mimicked the real thing. Then I ran them side by side. The results were fascinating.

It was genuinely difficult to distinguish one from the other. Both the original Ovilus and the software copy produced the same kind of responses: disjointed, occasionally interesting, sometimes eerily "*accurate*"—but entirely unprovable.

Even my stripped-down, sensorless clone was "*accurate*" a few times. The illusion held up. And that's the problem. The device didn't need a ghost. It didn't even need input. It just needed belief. A little randomness, a recognizable word, and a willing audience were all it took to pass as meaningful.

In the end, the Ovilus wasn't a communication tool. It was a confidence trick—one powered not by spirits, but by our own human pattern-seeking minds. Now I will admit that it's been years since I even held an Ovilus. Newer models might have changed. Maybe they now offer legitimate sensing (*do your own testing*). But even if that were the case, the concept of choosing words based on environment just seems… absurd.

SPIRIT BOX - GHOST BOX - FRANK'S BOX

The next device I turned my attention to was one that had been gaining traction among investigators for all the wrong reasons: the Spirit Box—also known as a Ghost Box, or occasionally, Frank's Box.

Its origin story is murky, but its function is simple: a

modified radio that scans through broadcast frequencies at high speed, producing chopped-up bits of music, news, talk shows, and static. And in that noise, many ghost hunters claimed to hear voices. Real ones. Spirits, they said, speaking through the static—answering questions, calling out names, delivering warnings. It was a seductive idea. But a dangerous one.

What troubled me wasn't just the faulty logic behind the device—it was how widely it was being used, and the damage it was doing. I saw teams enter private homes, Spirit Box in hand, and confirm for frightened families that they were not just imagining things—they were being haunted. Sometimes violently.

These weren't theatrical ghost tours. These were people— some with children—genuinely afraid for their safety, sometimes even selling their homes, and all of it, based on the garbled sputter of a hacked radio.

Whether you believed in the device or not, encouraging that fear—fueling it with pseudoscience—is inexcusable. It wasn't investigation. It was exploitation, and I wanted to prove it. But testing the Spirit Box wouldn't be easy. The claims were vague, and the results subjective.

What I needed was a way to separate cause from coincidence—to compare what users thought they were hearing to what was actually being broadcast. My solution was a device called Software Defined Radio (SDR)—a USB tuner that, when paired with decoding software, could monitor and record nearly the entire FM band at once. In real time. With this device, I could not only capture the raw output of a Spirit Box session, but I could also go back and match each audio fragment based on a timestamp, to its exact origin: a radio station, a DJ, an advertisement.

That was step one. I conducted a 30-minute Spirit Box session at home, recording both the Spirit Box output and the full FM band with synchronized timestamps. As expected, every *"ghostly"* word or phrase could be traced to a real broadcast. There was nothing mysterious about it—just fragments of familiar content, jumbled by the fast sweep of the tuner. I logged all of the stations and broadcasts that contributed to my recording. Complete with timestamps.

Next came step two—the field test. I was invited to join a

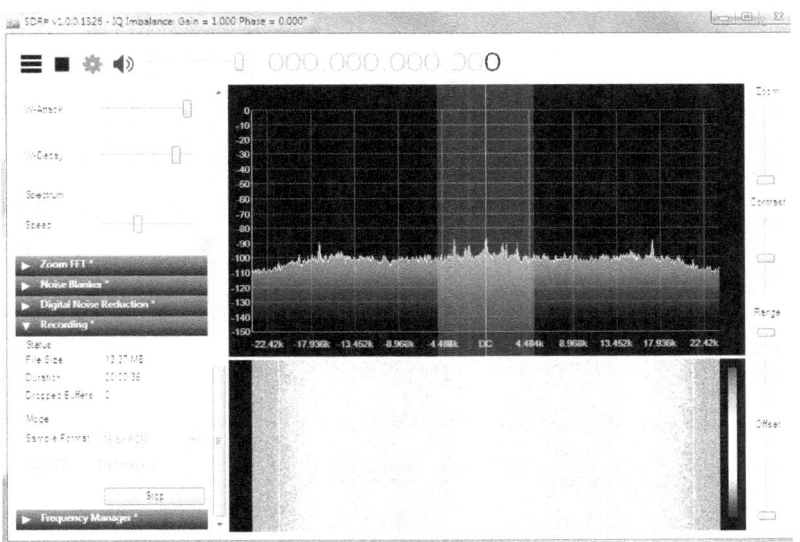

Software Defined Radio output showing spectrum of FM broadcasts.

group on a live investigation. This particular group was heavily invested in the Spirit Box phenomena. They brought the Spirit Box. I brought a portable speaker—and my 30-minute prerecorded session. At one point, without telling anyone, I swapped the live Spirit Box connected to my speaker with my playback device and hit play.

The team huddled around the speaker, asking questions, listening intently, and reacting with awe as "*voices*" responded in kind. They pointed out words they claimed tied directly to the location. Details they believed couldn't be coincidence. But they were. All of them.

They weren't listening to spirits. They were listening to the same radio static I'd recorded in my house days earlier—random snippets pulled from talk shows and commercials, now reimagined as evidence of the afterlife.

I published the results of the test. I documented every word. I showed the original sources. I made it as clear as I could: the Spirit Box wasn't detecting ghosts—it was exploiting our pattern-seeking brains,and still, it grew in popularity.

It was one of the most disheartening moments of my time in the field. Because when belief trumps reason, even the clearest evidence can be ignored.

GOOD TOOLS - BAD CONCLUSIONS

Not every piece of gear leading investigators astray is a blinking gimmick or a pseudo-scientific toy. Sometimes, the trouble lies in how legitimate tools are misunderstood—or worse, deliberately misused. Audio recording is a perfect example. On its face, a digital recorder is one of the most practical tools an investigator can carry. It's compact, reliable, and unobtrusive. It creates a permanent, timestamped account of what occurred—something useful not just in ghost hunting, but in journalism, research, even legal work.

Unlike so many other devices used in this field, an audio recorder doesn't pretend to detect ghosts. It records sound. That's it. And yet, even this simple, dependable tool has become entangled in paranormal mythology.

In recent years, there's been a curious shift: instead of seeking high-quality recorders, many investigators now chase the opposite—devices with poor sampling rates, low bit-depth, and high self-noise. The rationale? That more noise means more voices.

The thinking goes like this: a high-end recorder with noise cancellation might "*filter out*" the faint murmurs of a spirit voice. But a cheaper device, one prone to static, hiss, and distortion, might let those voices slip through.

On the surface, it sounds like a plausible defense— sacrificing clarity for sensitivity. But in practice, it's an invitation to pareidolia. When the background hiss of a noisy recorder becomes your primary data source, you're not investigating anymore. You're interpreting patterns in static— hearing what you want to hear. And the consequences are real. More noise means more ambiguity. More ambiguity means more chances for the mind to fabricate meaning.

I've met countless investigators who, rather than learning the physics of sound or the basics of acoustic analysis, double down on degraded audio and call it evidence. What's striking is how rarely spectrogram analysis is employed.

A spectrogram is a visual representation of audio frequencies over time—a standard tool in any real audio research. When paired with phonetic expertise, it can reveal whether a recorded sound even resembles human speech. Does it contain the spectral structure of a vowel? The transient burst of a consonant? Or is it just random noise with no linguistic pattern? The tools exist to make that call. But they're ignored in favor of gut feelings and suggestive whispers.

Back in 2014, I put this to the test in an accidental way. I

The discontinued Panasonic RR-QR8o
recorder I sold to Zak Bagans

listed an old Panasonic digital recorder on eBay—a clearance-rack special I'd bought for $11. It was loud, staticky, and practically useless. I figured I'd recover a few bucks. Instead, it sold for nearly $500. The buyer? None other than Zak Bagans. Yes, that Zak Bagans. I mailed it off to his home in Las Vegas, and while I don't follow his show, I wouldn't be surprised if that $11 relic later appeared on screen, marketed as some legendary EVP device. But here's the truth: no matter who's using it or how earnestly they believe, a noisy recorder doesn't make better evidence. It just makes more noise. And noise is the enemy of clarity—not its ally.

THERMAL IMAGING CAMERAS

Among the more legitimate tools often misapplied in paranormal investigation is the thermal imaging camera. Unlike some of the pseudoscientific devices that flood the market, thermal cameras—especially those made by FLIR—are real instruments with well-established applications. They've been staples in engineering, construction, and industrial maintenance for decades. Home inspectors use them to spot insulation gaps or leaking pipes. Electricians use them to locate overheating breakers. Factory safety teams rely on them to identify potential mechanical failures before they happen. They are, without question, valuable tools. But in the world of ghost hunting, their utility is frequently lost beneath a fog of misunderstanding.

Thermal cameras began appearing in paranormal television around 2004, most notably on *Ghost Hunters*, where they were portrayed as a cutting-edge means of detecting anomalies—cold spots, mysterious figures, vanishing heat signatures. At the time, the price tag made them rare. It wasn't until around 2010, when lower-cost consumer models entered the market, that their popularity exploded. Suddenly, groups across the world were using them, pointing them into the dark and declaring any shift in temperature as evidence of something unseen. But here's the problem: most of those using them had no idea what they were actually seeing.

A thermal imaging camera doesn't detect ghosts. It detects infrared radiation—heat—emitted or reflected by objects in its field of view. It doesn't show the temperature of "*air*" or measure spiritual energy. It shows surface temperature differences and visualizes them using a color gradient, usually mapped across a relative scale. Blue doesn't mean cold in an absolute sense—it means "*colder than the warmest thing in the image.*" Red or yellow may mean "*hotter*," but not necessarily *hot*. The scale shifts depending on what the camera sees, and without proper calibration or training, that context is lost. This leads to frequent misinterpretations. I've watched investigators point to a heat trail left behind by a person who just walked through a room and call it a ghost. I've seen others mistake reflective surfaces—like polished tile or glass—for heat anomalies because the camera registers ambient reflections, not direct emissions. One team I observed once insisted they had filmed a ghost peeking around a corner— only to discover it was the residual heat signature of a team member who had been leaning there minutes earlier. Even subtle changes in ambient airflow—caused by an HVAC vent or an open door—can produce shifting patterns that, to the untrained eye, appear supernatural. Thermal bloom, reflective heat bounce, emissivity errors—these are real, well-documented artifacts. But in the hands of a ghost hunter with little scientific background, they become omens.

Paranormal investigators often use thermal cameras not to measure, but to marvel. They aim them into empty hallways and wait for something unusual—without defining what they're looking for, or how they'll verify it when it appears. And like so many other tools in this field, the moment something ambiguous shows up on screen, belief rushes in to fill the gaps. But infrared doesn't lie. People do.

CLOSING THOUGHTS ON GEAR

By now, it should be clear that the problem isn't just the gear itself—it's the gravitational pull it exerts on the investigative process. Tools, especially in this field, have a way of becoming more than instruments. They become compasses. They steer the direction of inquiry, shape the questions asked, and—more often than not—predetermine the answers. And that's where the real danger lies.

It's easy to scoff at gadgets like the Ovilus or Spirit Box—easy to dismiss them as novelty items wrapped in pseudoscience. But even the more credible equipment—EM field detectors, audio recorders, thermal cameras—can send an investigation off course when used without skepticism or a clear understanding of what they're actually measuring. These tools don't just collect data; they shape how that data is interpreted. And when belief outweighs methodology, they become enablers of confirmation bias. That's not a flaw in the technology—it's a failure of intent.

Over the years, I've encountered dozens more devices. Some were ridiculous. Others, impressive in design. But all of them—regardless of sophistication—were prone to misuse. Laser grids. REM pods. Vibration sensors. Ion counters. I've seen baby powder treated like a data source. Motion sensors rigged with party lights. Geophones wired to buzzers. Teddy bears with antennas stitched into their backs, marketed as "trigger objects" for ghost children.

Each device came with its own made-up rules, each presented as if it were part of a legitimate scientific protocol. It wasn't. Not in the way it was being used.

Honestly, there's enough material on paranormal gear alone to fill another book. But the larger point is this: no matter how sleek, expensive, or popular, equipment is only as valuable as the investigative framework behind it. And in the world of paranormal research, that framework is almost always theatrical.

Devices are chosen for their spectacle, not their sensitivity. Their ability to impress a client, entertain an audience, or give the illusion of discovery. A blinking light becomes a breakthrough. A jumbled word becomes a message. A cold draft becomes a ghost. This isn't investigation. It's a feedback loop—performance and belief, reinforced by gadgets never designed to answer the questions being asked of them.

If that sounds harsh, it's because it needs to be. I'm not suggesting that technology has no place in the study of the unexplained. Quite the opposite. But the tools must *follow* the question—not lead it. Equipment should help test a hypothesis, not invent one. Otherwise, the pursuit becomes hollow—an echo chamber lit by LEDs and punctuated by static.

In the end, it's not the gear that's haunted. It's the thinking. Until that changes, the field will stay stuck—chasing shadows with toys and mistaking their noise for truth.

CHAPTER SIX

DEFINING EVIDENCE

Among the many words tossed around in the paranormal world, few are as misused—or as misunderstood—as evidence. It's a term that carries weight, one that should suggest credibility, substance, maybe even a glimmer of truth. But in the hands of many ghost hunters, it has been stripped of its meaning. Reduced to hashtags and file names, evidence is now anything that looks good on a social feed. I've watched investigators declare every anomaly, every spike on a meter, every draft of cold air as "*evidence*," uploading clips and screenshots like trophies from a battlefield no one else can see.

These digital offerings—grainy photos, muffled recordings, blinking lights—are often treated as foregone conclusions. Rarely are they questioned, analyzed, or even contextualized.

They are logged and left, buried in the cloud, forgotten as quickly as they were captured. It's not that these investigators are disingenuous. Most, in fact, are entirely sincere. But sincerity is not the same as scrutiny. And belief is not a substitute for process.

The classic definition of evidence is deceptively simple: anything that supports a claim. But even that generous framing requires a link—a logical, known connection between the data and the claim being made. A light through a window at midnight might be evidence that someone is home. It doesn't prove it—perhaps they stepped out and left the light on—but it supports the possibility. It's a clue grounded in what we already understand: people live in homes, people turn on lights. The connection, while not airtight, is at least anchored to reality. Now consider how that same logic breaks down in paranormal investigation.

Imagine a case in which a woman reports seeing shadowy figures moving through her hallway and insists that objects in her home are being moved without explanation. An investigation is launched, equipment deployed. Later, an investigator captures a faint voice on a recorder—childlike, whispering. They post it online with a caption: "*Evidence of the haunting.*" But is it? That voice, however eerie or unusual, has no direct relationship to the woman's claim. It's not evidence of shadows. It's not evidence of displaced objects. It is simply an unexplained sound—a data point without a clear connection to the phenomenon in question. Worse still, it's often declared evidence of a ghost.

Yet no one—despite decades of chasing and cataloging these recordings—has ever proven that electronic voice phenomena originate from the dead. There is no established, testable link between EVP and the spirit world – or even evidence of a spirit world at all for that matter. Without that connection, the claim collapses. The whisper on the tape may be strange, it may be intriguing, it certainly requires further investigation, but it is not evidence of the supernatural. It is data. Unexplained. Possibly misinterpreted. But data nonetheless, and until the bridge is built—until there is a demonstrable, repeatable pathway between the anomaly and the claim—it remains just that: unexplained.

I won't pretend I've always gotten it right. In my early years, I mislabeled plenty of data as evidence—too eager, too influenced by the moment. A stray sound. A strange reading. Sometimes it felt easier to assign meaning than admit uncertainty. But enthusiasm, however sincere, isn't the same as accuracy. What helped me course-correct wasn't just experience. It was distance.

I learned to stop asking *"What does this feel like?"* and start asking *"What does this support?"* because that's the real test. Does the data speak to the claim at hand or is it simply interesting noise, dressed up as relevance?

That shift—from emotional interpretation to contextual alignment—was critical. It forced me to see how often investigators zoom in on anomalies with the wrong lens. They dissect an unexplained sound but forget to ask if it has anything to do with the reported phenomena.

It's not the strangeness of the data that matters. It's the connection. When you're in the field, that distinction can get blurry. Especially when the house is dark, the equipment is rolling, and the team is leaning in with anticipation. But the moment you label something *"evidence,"* you're making a claim. And if that label is unwarranted, you're not just misleading others—you're misleading yourself. It's dangerous. Once you decide something must be evidence, you stop interrogating it. You stop asking better questions. Over time, that undermines the very integrity you're trying to build.

During my years of experimenting with coil-based microphones, I captured a handful of recordings that stood out—not for their theatricality, but for their resistance to explanation. One in particular has stayed with me: the sound of a woman crying. As you may recall, this was something I recorded at the Wayside Inn.

It was faint but unmistakable. Not ambient noise. Not a creaking pipe mistaken for breath. It was tonal, rhythmic, mournful. The room in which it was captured had a history— stories of a woman once confined there, a so-called spinster who spent her final years in solitude.

That backstory makes for a tidy narrative. Too tidy, maybe. But here's the thing: even with that convenient alignment between history and sound, I hesitate to call it evidence of a haunting.

What that recording gave me wasn't validation. It was questions. What produced this? What medium carried it? How old was the signal—if it was a signal at all? Was it acoustic? Electromagnetic? Residual? Refracted from another source entirely? Dozens of questions bloomed from that one sliver of data, each more important than the claim it was presumed to support. That's the part many investigators miss. They assume the strange must serve the story. But in cases like this, the story ends where the real work begins.

That recording didn't confirm a haunting. It became the subject of investigation itself. It redirected my focus—from validating the past to interrogating the present. What I had wasn't an answer. It was a lead.

Room 9 at the Wayside Inn remains, to this day, the most perplexing location I've ever investigated. Over time, it has yielded a variety of unexplained results—unusual field readings, structured audio anomalies, patterns that repeat in the absence of clear causes. But even there, in a space where the odd becomes routine, I've never allowed myself the shortcut of calling it haunted. Because to do that—to declare a haunting—is to claim far more than the data allows. It would require proof that a spirit world exists. Proof that consciousness persists after death. Proof that such entities can interact with our physical environment. And we don't have that. We never have.

So what can I say? Only this: Room 9 produces data that resists explanation. It's consistent. It's measurable. And for now, it's unknown. That's not a concession. It's the most honest representation I can give. Honesty may be the most radical act of all.

So then comes the question: how do you learn more about something unknown? How do you begin to dissect a phenomenon that arrives without context, without origin, and without a clear mechanism of action? There are several answers, but the first is simple—so simple it often gets overlooked. *Control and documentation.*

CONTROL AND DOCUMENTATION

If you're working with an unknown, then any variable—no matter how minor—might matter. The temperature of the room. The tilt of a sensor. The humidity in the air. When you're starting with zero clues, everything becomes a candidate for influence. Which means the only responsible approach is to treat the scene like a laboratory. Let's return to the woman crying.

That recording, faint and mournful, didn't just materialize. It was captured by a specific coil microphone, placed at a specific height, pointed in a specific direction, in a specific corner of the room. That detail matters—not just metaphorically, but mechanically.

Electromagnetic fields travel along specific paths—or axes. That's not just theory—it's basic physics. A coil can only "*hear*" a signal if it's properly aligned with the direction the field is moving. Think of it like the field of vision on a flashlight: the sensor only detects what falls inside its narrow beam.

In this case, the coil's range of sensitivity was tight—just about ten inches across. Had it been angled even slightly in a different direction, the signal might have passed right by, unnoticed. If you're serious about understanding the unknown, you start by removing the guesswork. You reduce the number of uncontrolled variables. You control what you can, and document the rest.

That night, I took notes not only on the positioning of the coil, but on the frequency characteristics of the recording itself. The crying—if that's what it was—occurred within a frequency band typical of a female human voice.

That was the starting point. But there was something else—something buried beneath the sound of the crying. A low, steady hum. It sat below the range of human hearing, around 16.7 hertz. Too low to be heard, but clearly visible on the spectrogram. And what stood out most was that it didn't match the familiar 60 hertz electrical hum you'd expect from standard wiring in a room like that. This was different. It began just before the crying started and faded out just after. It stood apart—out of place. Unexplained. A clue? Maybe.

That frequency became part of the puzzle. Not a conclusion, but a data point. I documented it. Along with every other active frequency. Along with environmental conditions: temperature, humidity, barometric pressure, even solar activity. Was it overkill? Possibly. But when you're chasing the unknown, overkill becomes insurance.

This is how you prepare for replication. If the event happens again, I'll know how to recreate the sensor positioning down to the inch. I'll know what to compare. What matched. What didn't. The original capture becomes a template—everything else becomes contrast. If it never happens again, I'll still know where I was pointing. And that's more than most investigators can say. Which brings me to the next requirement: *research*.

RESEARCH

Not the kind whispered between investigators over walkie-talkies or scribbled down on Facebook group threads. I mean real research. Peer-reviewed. Published. Grounded in the principles of tested science.

That doesn't mean I expect to open Nature and find a peer-reviewed article on disembodied voices captured through a spool of copper wire. But the goal isn't to confirm the anomaly—it's to contextualize it.

When something unexplained happens, the first step isn't to label it. It's to ask: *"Does any known science even come close to explaining this?"* Even a brush with established theory is better than jumping to conclusions.

So I'd dive into the literature—not looking for ghosts, but for physics. I'd ask whether there were any known mechanisms, even fringe ones, that could explain the recording. Could sound be converted into electromagnetic signals under specific conditions? Are there natural systems capable of storing electromagnetic energy and releasing it later in a recognizable form? And what about overlooked environmental effects? Piezoelectricity. Telluric currents. Magnetostrictive reactions. These aren't paranormal ideas— they're scientific ones, known to exist, even if rarely considered in this context.

Sometimes the search comes up empty. Sometimes it leads to theories too unstable—or too abstract—to be useful. But occasionally, a fragment of possibility emerges. A principle that, if not conclusive, is at least relevant. And that fragment becomes the seed of an experiment. Because research is only half the process. The other half is testing.

Once you have a sample—like the woman's cry—and a

carefully documented environment, you have the raw materials for controlled experimentation. You return to the same space. You place the coil at the exact same height, angle, and position. Then you change one variable. Just one.

Maybe the axis shifts by five degrees. Maybe the surface beneath the coil changes. Maybe you add a Faraday shield to block outside interference. Each adjustment is a new trial. And each one, no matter how small, is a chance to catch the edge of a pattern.

This is where patience becomes currency. There are hundreds—possibly thousands—of variable combinations to consider. And each test takes time. But that's the process. That's what rigor looks like in a field desperate for shortcuts.

After dozens of tests, patterns may start to emerge. A spike here. A strange resonance there. A reaction that only shows up under one very specific set of conditions—and disappears under all others.

That's the signal. That's the difference between a fluke and a clue. Because once something repeats—once you can test it—it starts to become understandable. And when that happens, the question changes. You're no longer asking, *"What did I hear?"* You're asking, *"What causes this to happen—and under what conditions?"*

You're not proving a ghost. You're isolating a mechanism. And that's where real discovery begins—not in confirming what you believe, but in asking better questions.

EDUCATION

There's one more element—often overlooked—that plays a critical role in how we identify and interpret evidence: *education*. And I don't mean degrees or credentials. I mean an intimate understanding of the tools you're using and the techniques you're applying.

In paranormal investigation, nearly every team is armed to the teeth with cameras—digital stills, film, video, infrared, full spectrum. The gear varies wildly, but one thing is almost always true: the people wielding it rarely understand how it truly works. Sure, many know how to point and shoot. They can toggle exposure, adjust ISO, fiddle with focus. But that's interface knowledge. That's surface. It's the difference between knowing how to drive a car and understanding how the engine functions. What's often missing is fluency—the ability to look at an image and understand what the sensor was actually seeing.

We like to think of cameras as mechanical extensions of our eyes. They seem to reflect the same reality: light enters, hits a surface, and the image appears. But the truth is far more complicated. A camera is not an eye. It's a translator—taking the physical phenomenon of reflected light and converting it into a digital approximation. And like any translation, things get lost. Or added.

The sensitivity of the human eye surpasses even the most expensive consumer-grade sensors. And unlike cameras, our brains are constantly correcting for color temperature, compensating for contrast, and filtering out irrelevant stimuli. A digital sensor doesn't have that level of nuance. Instead, it relies on software—algorithms designed by manufacturers to enhance clarity, reduce grain, and boost dynamic range.

These improvements may produce a better photo. But in the context of anomaly detection, they're liabilities. Consider this: if a manufacturer's goal is to produce clean, marketable images, then the software is built to suppress outliers—those very aberrations an investigator might consider significant. That doesn't make the technology useless. But it means we need to treat it for what it is: *a biased system*, one that manipulates reality before presenting it back to us.

This is why education matters—not for prestige, but for precision. If you're using a camera in the field, you should know what kind of sensor it uses. CMOS or CCD? What kind of lens distortion does it introduce? Does it apply post-processing compression? What light wavelengths can it see—and which ones are clipped or ignored?

Most importantly, you should understand the failure modes. Under what conditions will this device give you a false positive? What kind of image artifacts does it produce in low light? How does it handle motion blur or internal reflections? Without that knowledge, you're not collecting evidence. You're collecting guesses—filtered through a system you don't fully understand. I learned the importance of technical literacy the hard way—by chasing ghosts in other people's photographs.

Early in my investigative years, I took on a side project that I now see as a formative exercise. I started collecting *"famous"* ghost photographs—images that had made the rounds in books, lectures, and online archives—and tried to reverse engineer them. Not to disprove for sport, but to understand.

If something strange appeared in a photo, I wanted to know why. Was there a plausible cause rooted in optics, mechanics, or error? You might call it practice. I called it preparation.

One image stuck with me. It was a woman sitting on a bed, and above her—almost halo-like—arched bands of light floated in midair. They were semi-transparent, bright on one end, fading on the other, as if captured in motion mid-appearance. Like a glowing ribbon twirling across the frame, paused mid-flight. They didn't follow the lines of the room or the angles of the furniture, which added to their mystery. They were... misplaced. Suspended. Suspiciously poetic.

To avoid running afoul of copyright or dispute, I won't name the case or the location. But it was widely circulated. Allegedly, more than twenty investigators were present when the photo was taken. Only one camera captured anything. And of course, it was the camera held by the person most invested in the haunting.

For weeks I studied it, trying to recreate those arcs using plausible methods: long exposure, camera shake, reflective surfaces. Nothing matched. The light patterns seemed authentic. My gut told me there had to be a trick, but I couldn't find it.

Out of frustration, I contacted a friend—Asia (*pronounced Asha*), a seasoned professional photographer. I sent her the photo, expecting days of analysis. Her reply came in minutes. *"Thumbnail creases in the negative,"* she said. I blinked. *"What?"*

She explained: in film photography, if you mishandle a negative—press a thumbnail or curved object into it—you create a physical indentation. That indentation blocks light unevenly during the development process. The result, when printed, is a bright, curved arc that fades at the edges. It's not light in the room. It's light on the paper. And the camera, quite literally, had nothing to do with it.

Once she said it, I couldn't get it out of my head. The marks weren't floating. They were embedded. Etched. And they behaved exactly like a developer flaw would—showing only in select photos, from a single camera, at a specific angle. The negative was never released for independent review, which in hindsight is telling. In a room of twenty cameras, one caught magic. The rest caught nothing.

It was humbling. I didn't see it because I didn't know what I was looking at. I had no understanding of the chemistry behind development, or the physics of image exposure. But that detail—a simple arc—taught me a powerful lesson: sometimes the truth is physical. Not spiritual, and the devil, as always, is in the details.

That wasn't the last time a photo nearly fooled me. Another case came a few years later, during an online debate over a UFO photograph that had gained a decent following on paranormal forums.

The image showed a large, dark, saucer-like object— clearly landed in the woods. It appeared nestled between trees, resting on uneven terrain, with shadows stretching across the forest floor. The framing was tight, and the object's surface seemed to reflect the muted sunlight filtering through the branches. At first glance, it looked compelling. Too compelling.

There were no obvious signs of digital manipulation—no telltale edge artifacts or inconsistent lighting. And because the object was grounded, not hovering, the usual arguments about propulsion or suspension didn't apply. But something still felt off. The scale, for one.

The UFO looked massive, yet there was no disturbance on the ground—no compressed brush, no displaced leaves, no visible weight. The answer came, again, not from speculation—but from the negative.

It's a detail many overlook: film negatives often contain metadata in physical form. With the original strip in hand, you can identify things like aperture, shutter speed, and most importantly, focal length. And in this case, that was the crack in the story.

The focal point on the negative was less than two feet. Which meant the camera had been focused for a close-up—not a wide shot across a clearing. The massive landed craft? A small object, most likely a model, staged between two carefully selected saplings. Forced perspective had done the rest. There was no need for fancy software. The truth was baked into the image itself. All it took was knowing where to look.

It was a reminder that carried over when I began seriously reviewing video evidence, where illusions are often disguised by motion. Unlike still images, video offers continuity—and continuity can be a liability for hoaxes.

VIDEO

The first thing I look for in video is coherence. Do shadows remain consistent? Does the lighting shift logically as the camera moves? If a figure crosses the frame, does its motion track with the background and perspective? Staged videos often crumble under these questions. A light will move but cast no shadow. A shape will flicker oddly around its edges. The visual language breaks down.

Compression artifacts are another red flag. Many videos are edited or enhanced before being shared, and those edits often leave fingerprints. Frame interpolation, masking, or poor export settings introduce ghosting, tearing, or pixel inconsistencies that can reveal tampering. These flaws rarely show at full speed, but frame-by-frame, they become visible— edges that vibrate, shadows that detach, or transitions that stutter unnaturally.

The audio that accompanies the video is just as telling. I'll often extract the sound from the clip and view it as a spectrogram. Natural ambient noise has continuity— footsteps, wind, insects. If those sounds cut abruptly, repeat, or disappear mid-motion, it's a sign. Even when the picture looks perfect, the sound can unravel it.

Not every anomaly is fraud. But every piece of evidence deserves the burden of investigation. And often, it's the smallest technical clue—a depth of field mismatch, a compression glitch, a skipped waveform—that tells the real story.

In the end, the question of evidence was never just about data. It was about discipline. About resisting the urge to rush toward answers simply because uncertainty felt uncomfortable. That kind of restraint isn't glamorous. It doesn't play well on television. But it's essential if you're after truth instead of applause. What I came to understand—often the hard way—is that evidence isn't a trophy. It's a responsibility.

When you label something as evidence, you're not just sharing a finding. You're making a promise. A promise that you've done the work, checked the variables, ruled out the obvious, and are offering something that can withstand examination. And more often than not, I found I was the only one in the room holding to that promise.

It can be lonely, asking harder questions in a culture that celebrates quick conclusions. Lonely to treat your findings not as validation, but as puzzles—things to be broken down, not just built up.

Over time, I started to see the divide more clearly: between those who wanted to understand the unknown and those who wanted to own it. I never found much community in that space. The deeper I went, the less I saw others following. Not out of malice or disinterest—but because the work is slow. It asks for patience. For humility. For comfort with "*I don't know*" as a legitimate and honest outcome. That doesn't trend well. And it doesn't sell gear. Still, I believed in it. I still do.

When I think back to recordings like the woman crying in Room 9, or the tangled mess of gear sprawled across my desk during coil testing, I don't see failure. I see movement. I see process. Each question led to another. Each answer brought limits with it. And within those limits, I found integrity. Because real evidence—useful evidence—doesn't point to a conclusion. It points to a question worth asking again. And maybe that's why I eventually found myself stepping back. Not because the search had no value, but because I couldn't pretend it was the same search everyone else was on.

I was looking for clarity. For a signal that wasn't distorted by ego or agenda. With all the noise this field can generate, that kind of silence started to feel like home.

CHAPTER SEVEN

HAUNTED HUSTLE

It was a warm spring night in a quiet house just outside Sanford, Maine. A small team of paranormal investigators was preparing for what they believed might be a breakthrough—an opportunity to document a case unlike any they'd encountered before. The homeowner, a woman we'll call *Alice*, had described a haunting of rare intensity: violent, recurring, and deeply personal. She said she'd been scratched, shoved, even thrown from her bed. She spoke of unseen forces that left her breathless and bruised. Her stories were vivid, punctuated with moments of terror that seemed too detailed to be fabricated. If they were real, they would rank among the most extreme claims any of us had witnessed.

The team moved through the house with a steady efficiency,

setting up cameras, audio recorders, motion sensors—every tool at their disposal. When the gear was in place, the lights went out. Alice sat at the center of it all, on the edge of her bed, cradling a stuffed animal against her chest.

Around her, in the darkness, the investigators waited. The room was still. Tense. Everyone held their breath. Then, about twenty-five minutes later, Alice let out a sudden, cry.

"Something just touched my face!"

Lights snapped on. The room exploded into motion. Investigators scrambled toward her, eyes fixed on the fresh red line now visible across her cheek. For a few seconds, there was real panic. They'd seen scratches appear before, but never this clearly, never this dramatically. Then, from across the room, someone spoke up.

"We got that on camera!"

One of the infrared cameras had been trained on Alice the entire time. The team gathered around the playback and watched as the infrared feed told the real story. As the group sat silently in the dark, Alice reached into the band of her wristwatch—something no one had thought to examine—and pulled out a sewing needle she'd hidden there. In not one but two attempts, she pressed it to her cheek and dragged it down with enough force to draw blood.

She tucked the needle into her pillow, careful to bury it deep into the stuffing, only then did she let out her practiced cry. The deception was undeniable. What seconds earlier had been hailed as proof of a violent haunting now looked like a clumsy stage act, exposed under the same cameras she thought would vindicate her.

When confronted, Alice didn't break down. She didn't apologize or offer an explanation. Instead, she did something far more telling: *she doubled down.* She said the demon made her do it. That was her defense. That was the story she chose to stand behind. And no amount of evidence—no recording, no eyewitness—was going to shake her from it. It might sound like an outlier, an isolated act of desperation. But it wasn't. Not really.

Fraud has always had a seat at the paranormal table. Sometimes it's subtle. Sometimes it's staged. But it's there— woven through the history of the field like a quiet, stubborn thread. What's rarer is anyone calling it out. Rarer still is anyone willing to do something about it.

There's a kind of cultural immunity around these moments. A reluctance to confront, to embarrass, to admit when someone inside the circle has broken the trust. Whether it's politeness, fear of backlash, or a desire to avoid internal conflict, the effect is the same: *fraud is allowed to fester.* And the longer it goes unchallenged, the more damage it does—not just to credibility, but to the people who come seeking truth, only to find illusion.

Teams across the country proudly share *"evidence"* that, to anyone with even a modest grasp of photographic analysis, was clearly altered. Shadows that moved in ways they shouldn't. Light anomalies perfectly centered in frame after frame. Apparitions that appeared too distinct, too symmetrical—too good to be true. And always, the ubiquitous orbs: floating specks of dust caught in the glare of an infrared beam, paraded across grainy screenshots like digital confetti. Some of it laughable. Some of it maddening. But all of it posted with a straight face—and received with open arms.

The reactions followed a predictable pattern: likes, shares, breathless comments. *"Incredible catch!" "Proof at last!"* Occasionally, someone would chime in with a note of skepticism—pointing out the inconsistencies, the photographic artifacts, the obvious signs of manipulation. But their voices were quickly drowned out by the chorus of believers. The ones who needed the story to be true.

This isn't a new phenomenon. It didn't begin with Photoshop or TikTok. The fabrication of ghostly images has been around almost as long as photography itself. The tools have evolved, but the motivations haven't. There have always been people willing to manufacture the extraordinary. And there have always been crowds eager to believe it—especially when it confirms a narrative they're already invested in.

Perhaps it's the pull of mystery. Or the deep, human longing to believe that there's more to the world than what we can measure. But in this field, belief often trumps scrutiny. And that's where the real damage begins.

I've seen cigarette smoke passed off as ectoplasmic mist. Dust motes mistaken for spirits. I've watched videos carefully staged with props and actors—complete with pre-scripted *"paranormal events"*—edited to resemble authentic encounters with the unknown. These weren't isolated stunts. They were deliberate productions, crafted to deceive. And the worst part? They worked.

These clips went viral. They generated followers. They secured speaking gigs, earned sponsorships, even landed television deals. Meanwhile, the teams doing the real work—the ones chasing down drafts, tracing power fluctuations, and asking uncomfortable questions—were dismissed as skeptics, or worse: killjoys. Because they didn't deliver the chills. They didn't feed the fantasy. But the truth doesn't need a smoke machine. It doesn't need a shaky camera or a carefully timed bang in the silence. What it needs is patience. Rigor. A willingness to accept that most of the time... *nothing happens.* That's the hardest truth for most people in this space to confront. And for the frauds, it's the crack in the door. The weakness they exploit.

GHOST PHONE

In the summer of 2011 I received a call from a friend—let's call her *Mary*—a founding member of a Southern Maine research group I'd met a few months earlier. She was heading down to Massachusetts for an overnight investigation in the Freetown State Forest and wanted to know if I'd join. She didn't need to ask twice.

Freetown had a reputation. A stretch of woods with a long catalog of strange reports: phantom lights, vanished hikers, stories of ritual activity whispered through decades. It was the kind of place that drew investigators the way deep water draws gravity.

The event was hosted by a man we'll call Jay—the same person who had organized a convention where Mary and I first met several months earlier. Jay had risen fast in the local paranormal scene. In just a few months, he'd gone from a complete unknown to a minor celebrity. His name came up constantly. Too constantly. Everyone seemed to have a story about him.

According to those who'd investigated with him, his cases were never quiet. Activity followed him like weather. Meters spiked. Recorders picked up whispers. People came back from his investigations visibly shaken, talking about chills, voices, and flashes of movement. To hear them tell it, Jay didn't just study the paranormal—he attracted it.

Roughly eight months earlier, Jay hadn't been leading investigations. He'd been on the other end of the call—asking for help. That's how Para-Boston and I first met him. Back then, he was the one claiming to be haunted. According to his emails, his home had become a hotbed of activity: cold spots, slamming doors, shadow figures, even a refrigerator that, he claimed, opened on its own. The possibility of what this case might allow us to uncover was thrilling.

We brought a full team to his house. Jay and a friend—let's call him Jake—were there that night, mostly hanging in the background. They slipped in and out, stepping outside now and then—for a smoke, for a phone call, for one reason or another. Each time, some piece of equipment stirred. A K-II meter flickered. A motion detector chirped. A device somewhere registered just enough to make people take notice. Then Jay and Jake would drift back in, easy, unbothered, as though nothing at all had happened. It became a rhythm of the evening, one I noted quietly and set aside for later consideration.

Now, months later, I was driving into the Freetown State Forest to meet Jay and Jake again. But the roles had shifted. They weren't the *haunted* anymore. They were the hosts.

Jay's family owned a lumber business that operated within the forest, which gave him access to roads and trails that were typically gated at night. He'd turned that access into a business of his own—offering guided nocturnal excursions for paranormal groups, complete with SUVs, hand-drawn maps, and a ready-made narrative of local hauntings. The price? Three hundred dollars a night. *Cash only.*

We met just before dusk at a gravel lot on the edge of the forest. The SUVs idled in the falling light. Jay and Jake greeted people at the roadside like cruise directors. Guests unloaded cameras, recorders, EMF meters, flashlights, batteries. Introductions carried a buzz of nervous energy. By the time the sun dropped, the headlights snapped on, and we drove single-file into the forest's interior, the sense of expectation was as thick as the trees pressing closer around the road.

The forest swallowed us quickly. A half-mile in, the lead SUV veered off the main dirt road and onto a path that hardly deserved the name—rocks, ruts, branches that scraped the doors. The shocks groaned, tires spun, and the headlights caught nothing but trees, leaning in tighter with every turn. Eventually we stopped. What remained was silence and the kind of dark that feels physical, pressing against the glass, waiting to be let in.

We arrived at the remnants of an abandoned cabin, hidden deep in the woods. Jay claimed it was a site of past rituals—one of many whispered about in the area's folklore.

The Freetown State Forest had long been saddled with a grim reputation, largely fueled by a string of disturbing events that began in the late 1970s: reports of animal mutilations, scattered evidence of occult activity, and most infamously, the Carl Drew trial—a 1980 murder case involving a teenage girl, ritual elements, and a pimp-turned-suspect who quickly became the face of the region's supposed satanic undercurrent. Whether those events were truly connected or not, the association stuck. Places don't easily shake off stories like that. A cabin in the woods certainly fit the narrative. Small, empty, stripped of power and furniture, it stood like a husk in the trees—weathered and silent. You could feel the weight of past stories there, even if you didn't believe a word of them.

Mary's team moved efficiently. They'd done this before. Digital recorders were placed around the area. K-II meters lined up on large rocks that passed for a table. A full baseline sweep was conducted before anyone asked a question. No power meant no false readings from outlets or appliances. Just open air, layered with expectation.

One of Mary's standing rules was simple but effective: all cell phones off before an EVP session. No interference, no excuses. She moved through the group, checking for compliance. Even Jay, who was rarely seen without his Bluetooth earpiece simply nodded, and slipped it into his shirt pocket. With that, the EVP session began.

"Is anyone here with us?"
"Would anyone like to communicate?"

The K-II meter responded almost immediately. And not just occasionally—it pulsed in near-perfect rhythm with the investigators' questions. Ask, pause, spike. Ask again, spike again. It felt deliberate. Precise. The kind of responsiveness that's so rare, so clean, that you don't trust it.

Still, the area lit up—not just with the device, but with energy. You could see it on the investigators' faces. They were leaning forward, whispering their excitement. Some of them looked stunned. A few looked moved. For a moment, it felt like the line between belief and proof had narrowed to almost nothing. But Jay wasn't there. He'd wandered off before the session began.

When he returned, the others eagerly filled him in. The responsiveness, the timing, the rhythm. Jay just nodded. No smile. No real curiosity. No questions. It was subtle, but noticeable.

Later in the evening, a second session was held. This time, with Jay in attendance. As the questions rang out into the darkness, Jay stood silent, arms folded, expression unreadable. The K-II meter flared again—just as perfectly as before. Every spike matched a question. Every light, a beat in the conversation. It was uncanny.

Most EM field hits are fleeting, brief, messy, inconclusive. We chase patterns, and we rarely find them. But this? This was clean. Consistent. Mechanical. Was it possible Jay's reputation as a "paranormal magnet" was deserved?

In the week that followed, Mary's team did what serious investigators do: they review data. Hours of footage, audio logs, baseline readings—nothing was left unchecked.

Somewhere deep in that process, while combing through the session at the cabin, they caught something odd. A sound on video. Barely audible. Faint, but rhythmic—a high-pitched pulse that coincided with every spike on the K-II meter. That's when they called me.

Because of my background in frequency analysis, they asked me to take a closer look. With spectrum analysis software, I isolated the anomaly, and almost immediately a pattern emerged—unmistakable: 22 hertz.

To most people, that number wouldn't raise an eyebrow. But to anyone familiar with telecommunications, it stands out. 22 hertz is a known pulse frequency emitted by GSM (*Global System for Mobile Communications*) cell phones—specifically those operating on the IDEN network—during a process called a tower handshake. That's when a phone, even while

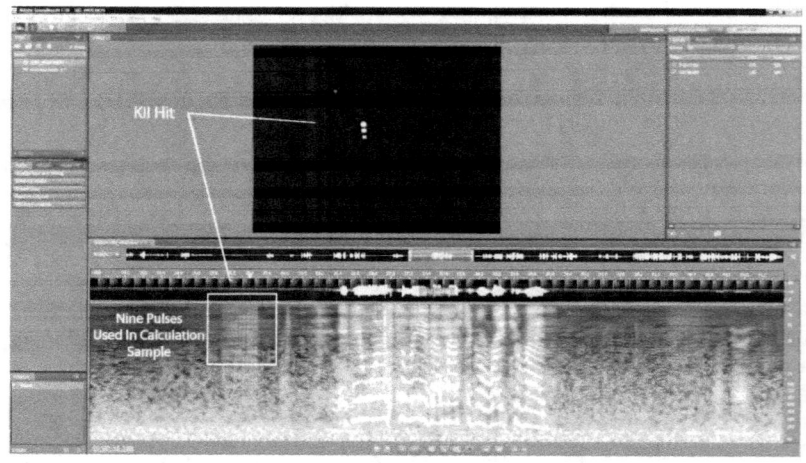

Spectrogram of cell phone signal
Photo by Michael Baker 2010

idle, sends out a brief burst of energy to check in with the nearest cell tower and maintain its signal. The IDEN network, at the time, was primarily used by Blackberry and Nextel phones.

In plain terms: the sound wasn't a ghost. It was a phone doing exactly what it was designed to do.

THE RETURN

The investigation at the cabin site had been unusually precise, strangely responsive—and now, increasingly suspicious. The events had been too clean, too cooperative. Questions were no longer optional.

Now that they knew what to look for, the investigation team decided to return the following weekend—this time with a different approach and tighter controls. I brought a Faraday cage. For the uninitiated, a Faraday cage is a grounded enclosure made of conductive material—essentially, a shield against electromagnetic interference. No signals in. No signals out. They're used in labs, clean rooms, and even the doors of microwave ovens. The one I brought was homemade: copper mesh-lined, small enough to carry, and built specifically to block high-frequency signals—especially those used by cell phones.

The test was simple: if the K-II meter responded inside the cage, we'd have something worth losing sleep over. But if it stayed silent—if the cabin itself failed to produce any spikes at all—then we'd have another kind of answer.

That night, we returned to the trail. The same forest. The same clearing. The same foundation, quiet and still beneath the trees—another $300. But this time? *Nothing*. No spikes.

No flickers. No bursts of light. The K-II meter inside the Faraday cage stayed dark. So did the one outside.

The difference was almost theatrical. The place didn't just feel quiet—it felt restrained. Like someone had pulled back the curtain and walked offstage. I couldn't prove anything. Not yet. But the silence spoke volumes. It felt intentional. And then—the break came.

During the investigation, Jay had mentioned—casually— that he'd just upgraded his phone. Mary, half-joking, asked if she could have his old one. It was a model she liked, and to her surprise, Jay handed it over with an easy grin. That was that. Or so it seemed.

Three days later, Mary called me. Her voice, this time, wasn't playful. Buried in the call history on Jay's phone, she'd found something we hadn't expected: a contact labeled *Ghost Phone*. Outgoing calls—multiple—each timestamped to the exact moments the K-II meter had lit up during the investigation a week and a half earlier. Not approximately. Exactly.

The illusion hadn't just been suspected. It had been orchestrated. And now, we had the proof: Jay had been triggering the K-II meter remotely.

The method was calculated. His Bluetooth earpiece—the one he had '*turned off*'—was still live. Hidden in his pocket, it stayed connected. With one discreet press through his shirt fabric, the signal fired. Launching a call to the "*Ghost Phone*" contact and an immediate hang-up.

The K-II meter reacted. And the illusion was complete. I called the number listed as "*Ghost Phone*" contact several times. No answer. No voicemail. Just silence.

When confronted, Jay and Jake denied everything. Of course they did. They offered up a disjointed catalog of excuses, the most creative being that the phone was *"voice activated,"* and perhaps Jay had unknowingly triggered it by uttering the phrase *"ghost phone"* during the investigation.

It would've been laughable, if it hadn't been so transparent. That moment fractured whatever trust had existed.

From then on, our interactions were stiff, transactional. Jay grew defensive. Jake stopped returning calls entirely. They knew we knew. And we knew exactly what we'd been a part of.

That investigation remains a turning point for me—not just because of the trick itself, but because of what it revealed about the ecosystem of paranormal research. It exposed a

The infamous 'Ghost Phone' used on the night of the cabin investigation.
Photo by Michael Baker 2010

blind spot that too many investigators still refuse to acknowledge.

There are teams who pride themselves on their diligence. They debunk cold spots. Trace drafts. Investigate faulty wiring and structural creaks before even entertaining the idea of the unexplained. That level of scrutiny is vital. But when fraud comes from within the group—when the deception isn't from a homeowner, but from the person holding the other end of the flashlight—skepticism vanishes. Especially on joint investigations.

There's an unspoken rule in many corners of the paranormal world: *if someone's in the field, they must be here for the right reasons.* There's a presumption of integrity—a built-in trust among colleagues that renders them almost immune to suspicion. Fraud, it's assumed, is something that happens *to* investigators, not *by* them. But that assumption is flawed. Worse—it's dangerous.

The more I watched this dynamic unfold, the clearer it became. The problem wasn't just that fraud existed. It was that no one wanted to believe it could.

Investigators held a reasonably high bar for ruling out natural explanations. But when it came to human ones? That bar all but disappeared. All it took to earn credibility was a logo on a t-shirt and a few well-placed buzzwords. Once someone was "*in*," the questions stopped.

Jay wasn't the only person I saw blur the line between truth and theater. But his was one of the rare cases where the deception left a trail—something you could point to, analyze, and verify. Most of the time, you're left with suspicion. A too-perfect response. A moment that feels a little too rehearsed. And no one wants to be the one who speaks up—especially when the clip might end up in someone's highlight reel, captioned as *"evidence."* But silence, I learned, carries its own consequences.

Every faked response. Every staged EVP. Every manipulated meter reading—it all chips away at the credibility of the field. With each lie passed off as truth, it becomes harder for sincere investigators to be taken seriously. Harder for genuine anomalies—whatever their nature—to rise above the noise. And that's what stayed with me. It wasn't just the deception. It was how *eager* people were to believe it.

That kind of blind trust doesn't stop at local teams. It travels up the ladder—to the personalities with book deals, podcast empires, and national TV contracts. If anything, the higher someone climbs, the fewer questions they're asked. Visibility seems to grant immunity. Because calling out fraud isn't just uncomfortable—it's inconvenient. Especially when the person responsible commands an audience. Even when you have the truth, it's strange how little impact it seems to make.

Take *Most Haunted*, the British TV show that, to its credit, once tried to do the right thing. Parapsychologist Ciarán O'Keeffe suspected the show's resident medium, Derek Acorah, was embellishing his experiences—if not fabricating them outright.

So he set a trap, feeding Acorah a pair of fictional spirit names: *"Rik Eedles"* and *"Kreed Kafer"*—thinly disguised anagrams for *"Derek Lies"* and *"Derek Faker."* Sure enough, Acorah *"channeled"* both of them, live on camera.

It should've been career-ending. And for him, it was. He was quietly let go, and the show pivoted. Producers leaned harder into skepticism. They aimed for integrity. But it came at a cost. The audience began to fade. Ratings slipped. The show, once a cultural mainstay, limped toward cancellation. Viewers hadn't tuned in for caution or critical thinking. They came for chills. And when *Most Haunted* stripped away the illusion, it also broke the spell.

Across the Atlantic, *Ghost Hunters* faced a different scandal: a viral clip of a jacket hood being pulled—visibly, inexplicably—in a way that suggested someone behind the scenes had staged it. The moment circulated widely. Fans speculated. Critics weighed in.

The show runners said nothing. No retraction. No explanation. Just silence. The show continued, unbothered. Same cast. Same format. Same steady ratings, and it worked. *Ghost Hunters* ran for nearly many years after that—spawning spin-offs, brand partnerships, conventions. The ghost kept haunting, and the audience kept watching. Why? Because people don't tune in for the truth. They say they do. They *want* to believe they do. But what draws them back week after week is the adrenaline, the comfort, the familiar cadence of spooky music and whispered suspense.

When *Most Haunted* peeled back the curtain, the magic disappeared. When *Ghost Hunters* left it intact, the fantasy endured. That's the trick: exposure breaks the illusion. Denial sustains it. We see it everyday in political culture. And it's a strange, bitter lesson for anyone who values the truth.

In this space, the shows that refuse to confront fraud often outlast the ones that do—because they protect the emotional investment of their audience. They preserve the mythology. They let people believe that ghosts are real, that investigators are trustworthy, and that the next hallway might finally reveal the proof they've been waiting for. In the world of paranormal television, it's not about what *is* real. It's about what *feels* real. And that difference can mean everything.

From the beginning, *Ghost Adventures* built its reputation on volume. The pacing was frantic, the tone breathless, and the reactions—well, they were something else entirely. Every EVP was a growl. Every cold spot, a demonic force. Every building was billed as the *most* haunted they'd ever seen. The show was theatrical, unrestrained, and—at times—so exaggerated it veered into parody and yet (*again*)… it worked. The performance was the hook. The chaos kept people watching. But as the seasons went on, I found it increasingly difficult to take seriously.

The evidence came thick and fast in those early episodes—shadows slipping past doorways, disembodied voices on cue, and in one unforgettable moment, a brick launched itself across a basement floor. An actual brick.

The scene was pure frenzy: shouting, shaky camera work, panicked footsteps echoing down the corridor. And then—just as quickly—it was over. No pause. No analysis. No examination of the pile it supposedly came from. Just a hard cut—and on to the next.

It was, by all appearances, a watershed moment. If a brick *really* moved on its own, that would be extraordinary. You'd expect everything to stop. Measurements to be taken. Angles reviewed. But none of that happened. And that—more than the brick itself—is what stayed with me. Because if something truly inexplicable had occurred, they had an obligation to treat it with gravity. They didn't. They treated it like set dressing. A prop. A scare. So I did what any skeptical investigator would do: I tried to replicate it. A fake brick. A length of fishing line. A few trial runs. It didn't take long. Within minutes, I had recreated the moment almost exactly. Same arc. Same timing. Same chaos. And once I saw how easily it could be done, everything changed. I stopped seeing shows like *Ghost Adventures* as investigations. I started seeing them as performances—choreographed dramas in ghost-hunting costumes. Entertainment, not inquiry. Emotion in place of evidence. The fear was real—but only for those willing to stop asking questions.

Back in 2008, I appeared briefly on *Ghost Hunters*— Season 4, Episode 11—after investigating an inn in Yarmouth Port, Massachusetts.

I'd experienced a few genuinely strange things there: odd readings on my equipment, unexplained breathing sounds, and what I still believe was a moving shadow.

The producers interviewed me for over 40 minutes. I described everything I'd seen and heard. But when the episode aired, my contribution was reduced to a few seconds of screen time. And not just shortened—but *reshaped*.

They used my comments to support activity in a room I had never mentioned. The details didn't matter. The footage was molded to fit a narrative they had already chosen. No one from the show contacted me during filming. None of the other witnesses were asked for input. No one fact-checked anything. Because the story had already been written. They just needed the footage to match it. Back then, I was still a little naïve. I thought I was helping a team uncover something meaningful. I didn't realize I was just another part of the script. After that, everything changed.

Michael Baker conducting an electric field experiment at *The Colonial House Inn* in 2008. The experiences encountered during this experiment were used as witness testimony on *Ghost Hunters*.

Not all evidence is fabricated. I still believe that. But when every scare lands like a cue from a horror movie—when every location delivers on command—it's worth asking whether what you're watching is investigation, or just entertainment dressed up in night vision. And it wears on you. Not just the fakery itself, but the way people respond to it—or refuse to.

You can walk them through the footage, show them the inconsistencies, line up the timestamps—and they'll still shrug. "*Well, maybe it's real*," they say. Or worse: "*Even if it's fake, at least it gets people interested.*" That logic always struck me as dangerous. Because if you actually care about the work—if you're serious about understanding what's *really* happening—you can't excuse deception just because it comes with dramatic music and a jump cut. You can't build a meaningful foundation on half-truths and then act surprised when no one takes you seriously. But plenty of people were happy to make that trade. They didn't want uncertainty. They wanted belief. They wanted the version of reality that comforted, not the one that questioned. And some of them took it even further.

There were those who faked activity and then stood in the dark pretending to be stunned by it. Who planted devices, nudged results, and then joined the group in wide-eyed disbelief—like their surprise somehow absolved them of the lie. As if innocence could be mimed. But it didn't look honest. It looked rehearsed. And that's when everything gets muddy.

When you can't tell who's performing and who's genuinely curious, the trust that holds a team together starts to unravel. You share less. You second-guess more. Every result becomes suspect. Every motive, a little harder to read. That was the shift for me.

I stopped sharing freely. Stopped assuming everyone was chasing the same goal. I didn't want to become the bitter skeptic in the corner—but I also couldn't ignore what I'd seen. Because it mattered. It still does.

Fraud isn't just a minor irritant in this field. It's a kind of rot. It seeps into the foundation. It undermines real inquiry, poisons public trust, and slowly drives out the people who actually care. I'd come in chasing evidence. I stayed chasing clarity. But I was leaving with one important question. *Was it still worth it?*

CHAPTER EIGHT

STORIES WE TELL OURSELVES

Over the thirteen years I spent investigating the unexplained, one question trailed me more than any other. It arrived in quiet conversations, in interviews, at panels and lectures—curious, sometimes skeptical, often hopeful:

"Do you believe in ghosts?"

It sounds like an easy question, the kind you might answer with a shrug and a smile. But it never was. Not for me. Part of the difficulty lies in the word itself. *Ghost.* It evokes something specific—an image we've all inherited. A pale figure. A whisper down an empty hallway. A moan from the attic. But press harder, and you'll find the definitions splinter. For some, a ghost is the soul of the departed, lingering between worlds. For others, it's a flicker of emotion, a memory held in place. A demon. A glitch in time. A trick of the mind. Ask ten people and you'll get ten interpretations.

So if you mean the classic specter—the translucent figure slipping through walls, moaning at midnight—then no, I don't believe in that. I don't believe in the Hollywood ghost, in the chain-rattling phantoms of old novels or horror franchises. But if you're asking whether people experience *something*— something they can't explain, something that shakes them, unsettles them—then yes. Without hesitation. I believe they do. I've had those moments myself. I've watched shadows move against still air.

I've heard voices—clear, articulate, impossible—with no one nearby. I've seen objects shift in rooms no one had entered. I've captured recordings that defy every conventional explanation I could summon. And I've listened to others— people I trust—describe similar encounters with a kind of trembling clarity that's hard to dismiss. What I don't believe in is the rush to certainty.

That's what I've seen most often. Something strange occurs, and before the echo fades, it's been labeled: *a ghost.* No pause. No inquiry. Just a well-worn narrative slipping into place. And I understand why—it's comforting. Certainty always is. It spares us the discomfort of ambiguity. It tells us we've seen this before, and we already know what it means.

I once heard John Lennon say in an interview, *"God is a concept by which we measure our pain."* That line stuck with me. Not because of its theology, but because it captures something essential about belief: *we reach for it when we feel unmoored*. When life slips off its rails, we search for explanations that can give it shape again—divine, paranormal, or otherwise.

And for generations, ghosts have been part of that architecture. They show up in folklore, in film, in the stories we whisper to each other on long drives or late at night. So when something unexpected happens—a sound, a chill, a shadow—we reach for the familiar.

We call it a haunting. But what we're often reaching for isn't a fact—it's a story. One we've been told a hundred different ways. One that feels easier than sitting with the unknown.

What worries me isn't belief. It's *certainty*. That hard edge of conviction that shuts the door on further inquiry. The idea that, because something looks and feels like what we've seen in movies, it must be the same. But that leap skips too many steps. It ignores the extraordinary strangeness of the natural world. It assumes we've already uncovered everything there is to know. We haven't.

Science—especially in its deeper corners—is filled with phenomena that are unintuitive, even bizarre. Quantum particles that defy our understanding of motion. Biological processes that behave unpredictably under stress. We live in a world where known mysteries outnumber solved ones. So why should we assume that everything we don't yet understand must be supernatural?

During the filming of *14 Degrees*, one of the investigators said something that made the final cut: "*Anything we can't find a rational answer for is paranormal.*" At the time, I understood the impulse behind the statement. But even then, it felt like a mistake.

The world doesn't divide so neatly. It isn't binary—explained or ghost. There's a wide and complicated terrain between those poles. A space where the strange and the plausible overlap. A space that requires patience, humility, and, above all, curiosity. That's where I've always tried to stay. In the quiet, unsettled middle. Where the stories begin.

Over the course of my research, one truth asserted itself again and again: the story doesn't begin and end with the environment. Any serious investigation into the unexplained must examine not only the setting, but every variable in play—including the most unpredictable one of all: *the human mind.*

Yes, atmospheric conditions matter. Electromagnetic fields, temperature fluctuations, radiation levels—these are all worth measuring. They offer data points, tangible fragments of a larger puzzle.

The tools we use to measure them matter too. Understanding how an instrument behaves, where it excels, and where it fails—that's foundational. Anomalies mean little if your equipment can't be trusted. But in the eagerness to catalog environmental factors, we often overlook a far more influential component: *the observer.*

The brain is not a camera. It doesn't simply record reality. It edits, filters, and translates. It weaves together impressions into coherent stories, even when the raw data is incomplete or contradictory. And under the pressure of stress, fear, or anticipation, that mental storytelling becomes even more prone to error.

PERCEPTIONS

Michael Baker lecturing in
Bridgewater, MA. 2011

That's why I found myself returning, time and again, to the subject of perception. How do we see? How do we *think* we see? What happens in the gap between sensation and belief?

I gave small lectures on the topic—informal talks for investigators and curious laypeople—often using simple demonstrations to illustrate how easily we can be fooled.

One of my favorites was about peripheral vision. I'd ask for a volunteer and have them stand facing a wall, eyes fixed on a single point. No turning their head. No darting glances. Just a steady gaze. Then, from behind, I'd have two people walk slowly toward either side of their visual field.

The instructions were straightforward: as soon as the volunteer noticed movement at the edge of their vision, they were to call out, "*stop*." Once they did, I'd ask a follow-up: *describe what they saw*. The clothing. The colors. Any physical details. In every case, the answers were wrong.

Participants could rarely identify the correct shirt color—sometimes not even the presence of a logo or a long sleeve. It wasn't a trick. It was a revelation: they simply *hadn't seen* what they thought they had. And the science behind it is well known.

Peripheral vision evolved not for detail, but for detection. The outer edges of our visual field are populated by rod cells—sensitive to light and movement, but blind to color and fine resolution. That's why we notice a flicker or flutter in the corner of our eye, but can't say what caused it. It's how we spot a predator in the underbrush—or think we do.

So when the brain receives only fragments, what does it do? *It fills in the gaps.* It tells a story. It creates a version of reality that feels complete, even when it isn't, and that's where things get shaky. Especially in the dark.

The mind is a skilled architect of illusions. Given just a few fragments, it can construct a version of reality that feels not only plausible, but complete. It draws from a well of context, memory, expectation, and emotion. And in the right setting—low light, heightened tension, the kind of atmosphere common in the places we investigated—that process can yield something remarkably persuasive. So persuasive, in fact, that even the most rational observer might swear they saw something that simply wasn't there. This is how a flicker at the edge of vision becomes a ghost story. A shadow, a shifting shape—something glimpsed just out of view. Not because someone is lying, but because the brain is doing what it has always done: making sense of the incomplete.

In paranormal research, this isn't just interesting—it's

essential. Because before you jump to the unknown, you have to ask the most fundamental question of all: What exactly did you see? And perhaps more importantly: what didn't you?

The limitations of human vision extend well beyond the periphery. We're not built for darkness. Our eyes operate within a narrow slice of the electromagnetic spectrum. We can focus on only one depth field at a time—everything else falls into blur. But the most compelling limitation isn't optical. It's cognitive. It's what happens after we see something—how we interpret the image, and what meaning we assign to it.

Humans are exceptional pattern-seekers. We're hardwired to find order in chaos. And nowhere is that instinct more pronounced than in our ability to recognize faces. We do it constantly—in clouds, in the folds of curtains, in water stains and window reflections. I've seen people swear that a blurry photo of dust captured the face of a child. That a cabinet's reflective glare revealed a full-bodied apparition. And the thing is—they believed it. They weren't being dishonest. They weren't exaggerating. They saw those faces because our brains are exquisitely tuned to look for them.

The reason is evolutionary. Recognizing a face—friend or threat—before it fully emerged could mean survival. In some ways, it still does. That's why you can identify someone from the curve of a cheek in a blurry photo, or from the outline of their walk across a crowded room. But that same sensitivity comes with a cost. We don't only see faces when they're present. We see them when they're not. This is pareidolia—the anthropomorphic tendency I mentioned earlier.

A pair of shadows becomes eyes. A smudge arcs into a

smile. A faint outline suggests arms, shoulders, even posture. The brain stitches these fragments together with astonishing speed and certainty, turning visual noise into something familiar. Something human. And once you see the face, it's nearly impossible to unsee.

In paranormal circles, this presents a serious challenge. Investigators often work with low-resolution video, infrared imagery, and grainy, shadow-drenched environments—the exact conditions in which pareidolia thrives. Add a whispered backstory—"a little girl died in this room," "a man hanged himself in the basement"—and the mind begins to prime itself for meaning. Every reflection, every blur, every digital artifact becomes suspect. In those moments, belief becomes inseparable from perception. And the image, however false, begins to feel like truth. It's not about gullibility. It's about being human. That's why I always urged people to pause, to look again, and to ask a question too often ignored in the moment: *"Would I still see it if I didn't expect to?"* The real challenge isn't capturing the unexplained—it's recognizing when your mind is filling in the blanks, and misperception isn't limited to vision.

Every one of our senses is prone to error. Touch is no exception. We like to think of touch as straightforward. A stimulus occurs; we feel it. But the process is far more complex. The human body is threaded with a vast network of sensory receptors, sending continuous streams of data to the brain. Most of that data is filtered out—background noise we never consciously notice. A shift in air temperature. The slow ebb of blood flow. A tingle, a twitch, a subtle cramp. We ignore it—until the setting urges us to pay attention. A creak becomes a step. A twitch becomes a touch. When you expect something to happen, the ordinary takes on meaning. In isolation, a minor muscle spasm in the shoulder can feel uncannily like a tap. A nerve firing in the leg might register as a poke. And when you're lying in the dark, primed to anticipate contact, the mind is quick to translate those signals into something external. Something meaningful.

Over the years, I've spoken with dozens of people who swore someone touched them in the night. A hand on the arm. A tug at the sheet. The weight of someone settling next to them. And I never doubted that they *felt* something. But more often than not, the explanation wasn't paranormal. It was anatomical.

Here's one I know firsthand: lie on your side in just the right position—one arm pinned beneath your body, your heart pressed gently into the mattress—and wait. After a few minutes, the circulation begins to slow. The arm tingles. The chest pulses. That subtle, rhythmic thump—your own heartbeat—starts to feel like something shifting next to you. Or breathing. Or slipping into the bed. It's not a ghost. It's blood flow.

The somatosensory system—the brain's network for interpreting physical sensation—is remarkably adaptive. What it perceives is shaped not just by contact, but by focus, attention, and belief. Tune your awareness to a body part long enough, and even a benign sensation can become loaded with meaning. Add a little fear or anticipation, and that signal grows louder. More vivid.

There's even a phenomenon known as *tactile pareidolia*—a

cousin to the visual and auditory effects I've seen so often in the field. It's what happens when the brain, lacking clarity, fills in the blanks with familiar sensations. The soft drag of a blanket might register as fingers. A creak in the mattress as someone shifting their weight. A subtle breeze might be interpreted as breath. The experience is real. The feeling happened. But that doesn't mean the source was external. In many cases, it wasn't a presence. It was a moment—an entirely natural convergence of physiology and expectation that, together, created a powerful illusion. And in the stillness of a darkened room, where fear heightens every sense and silence amplifies every signal, illusion doesn't just feel like the truth. It *becomes* it. Even scent isn't exempt from misinterpretation.

SCENT

Over the years, I've spoken with dozens of people who've shared remarkably similar stories: the sudden, unmistakable trace of a familiar perfume. A specific cologne. A floral note tied to someone long gone. The acrid sweetness of a cigar once favored by a relative who'd passed decades earlier. They describe these moments vividly, sometimes through tears. The scent appears, unbidden. Potent. Fleeting. And then—just as suddenly—it's gone. No one else smells it. No evidence remains. But to the person experiencing it, the encounter is unmistakably real. And in a way, it *is*.

Scent is a curious thing—one of our most powerful senses, yet also one of the least understood and most susceptible to suggestion. Unlike sight or sound, which route through the brain's sensory hub—the thalamus—before reaching the regions responsible for recognition and emotion, scent takes a more direct path. It travels straight to the limbic system, the brain's emotional core—bypassing the usual sensory filters.

There, memory, mood, and sensation become deeply entangled. It's why the faintest aroma can pull you back to childhood in a single breath. A scent can transport. It can haunt. But that same neurological shortcut also makes scent unusually vulnerable to context and expectation.

The olfactory system doesn't just receive chemical signals—it interprets them. And when memory or emotion is running hot, the brain can simulate the experience of smell without any external stimulus at all. There's a name for this: *phantosmia*, or olfactory hallucination. It's not a glitch in the nose. It's a feature of the mind—a testament to the brain's ability to recreate sensory experiences based on association, memory, and mood.

Imagine the setting: You're in an old house. You've been told it's haunted. Maybe a loved one died there. Maybe you've been primed by stories—stories about how her perfume still lingers, or how he smoked that brand of cigar right up until the end. Then someone whispers, *"Do you smell that?"* And maybe you do. Or maybe you remember the scent so vividly that your brain fills in the blanks. Research bears this out. Numerous studies have shown that scent memory is extraordinarily responsive to emotional cues.

In one experiment, participants who were asked to imagine the smell of roses while viewing images of the flower activated the same brain regions as those exposed to actual rose oil. The brain, influenced by suggestion and imagery, generated the sensation without the stimulus.

In paranormal investigations, this effect can be magnified. Emotions are heightened. Expectations are primed. You're actively looking for signs. So when a faint aroma drifts by—whether it's mold, perfume residue, or a nondescript chemical note—your brain assigns it meaning. "*lilacs*", you think. "grandma's perfume." And the more personal that association is, the more real the scent becomes in your memory. It isn't fabrication. It's not a lie. It's not even irrational. It's just... human.

The mind is a master at closing gaps—especially when grief, nostalgia, or fear slip into the equation. When those forces converge, even the stillness of the air can feel weighted, expectant—haunted, in the quietest sense of the word.

LISTEN UP

If vision is the most visibly prone to misinterpretation, hearing may well outpace it in subtlety. Sound doesn't just register—it *persuades*. It bypasses analysis. Unlike sight, which we're trained to question, sound tends to arrive with authority. It feels intimate. Immediate. And in the dark, it can become conviction.

That's what makes auditory misperception such a potent force in paranormal investigations. The brain processes sound just as it does vision: by building patterns from incomplete input. In the realm of ghost hunting, this tendency manifests most clearly in a phenomenon known as *audio pareidolia*—the impulse to hear voices in static, whispers in the wind, meaning in noise. It's the auditory cousin of seeing faces in clouds. But in this case, the canvas isn't a sky—it's static. And the expectation isn't playful; it's purposeful. You're not daydreaming—you're hunting.

I've reviewed hundreds—likely a thousand—of these so-called EVPs: snippets of audio collected in quiet rooms, reviewed hours later in headphones, held up as proof of unseen voices. In almost every case, the investigator is convinced they've captured speech. Some offer transcripts. Others argue over phrasing. But when I analyzed these recordings using spectrograms—visual representations of sound—I saw what I suspected all along: *no identifiable speech*. No vocal patterns. No phonetic architecture. Just noise. And I don't say that to dismiss the people who made those recordings. On the contrary—I understand the impulse. I live with it.

I've had partial hearing loss since my early twenties. I know exactly what it's like to mishear a word, to chase a sound you think you recognize. It was that very uncertainty that led me to study spectrograms in the first place. I wanted a second opinion. A way to *see* what I could no longer fully trust my ears to hear. More investigators, I think, should have done the same.

In 2013, I published a short paper: *Linguistic Comprehension of Electronic Voice Phenomena: An Experiment in Auditory Perception Accuracy*. It was a modest study, but one I still stand by. The idea was to test how accurately people could interpret distorted speech—audio designed to mimic the murky, half-heard conditions so common in EVP recordings.

With help from my team at the New England Center for the Advancement of Paranormal Science, I recorded ten short clips. Each one contained actual spoken words—but whispered faintly, buried under ambient noise, or deliberately masked by layered environmental sounds.

The goal was to replicate the exact kind of audio often labeled as "*evidence*." We then played the clips for volunteers. No context. No coaching. Just raw playback. Their task was simple: tell us what they heard. The results were striking.

When I finally compiled the surveys, a pattern emerged— subtle at first, then undeniable. People didn't just want to hear something. They *needed* to. Even in the absence of clarity, even when the recordings were garbled or nonsensical, participants confidently supplied answers. And the less familiar or more ambiguous the phrase, the more their accuracy dropped. That alone wasn't surprising. But what did catch me off guard was the confidence behind those misinterpretations.

Participants didn't hedge or second-guess. They wrote their answers with certainty—sometimes even echoing one another, arriving at the same incorrect interpretation without realizing it. These weren't random guesses. They were *patterns*. Evidence of the brain doing what it's always done when faced with ambiguity: reaching for resolution, even where none exists.

That, in essence, was the point of the experiment. I wanted to test not just auditory accuracy, but susceptibility—how easily expectation and context could override reality. And the results confirmed what I had long suspected: many so-called EVPs weren't whispers from the dead. They were echoes of the living. Interpretive errors. Cognitive artifacts dressed up as truth. But misperception doesn't operate in a vacuum.

Context matters—a great deal more than most investigators are willing to admit. Where you are, what you've been told, the mood in the room, even the temperature of the air—these things don't just shape perception. They *guide* it. A drafty cellar in a centuries-old inn doesn't sound the same as a carpeted office suite. Creaking wood and the faint scent of mildew prime the mind for unease. Add dim lighting, a whispered legend, and a handheld recorder, and you've created the perfect storm.

Paranormal teams often excel at building that atmosphere. Whether intentional or not, they set the stage like seasoned performers: lights off, voices low, footsteps slow. They address the room as though something is listening. They ask questions and pause, waiting for silence to answer. It's immersive. Dramatic. Theatrical. And it works. Because when you *expect* a voice, even static can sound like a sentence.

There's an old saying: *when you have a hammer, everything looks like a nail.* In this world, when you believe you're in a haunted place, *everything* starts to sound like a ghost. A pop becomes a whisper. A breath becomes a message. And it's not fraud. It's not fakery. It's what human beings do—searching for patterns, reaching for meaning in the dark. That's what makes it so insidious. Most of the time, the error goes unnoticed. Even the listener doesn't realize it's happening.

It forced me to rethink the self-declared *"experts"* I'd met over the years—those who claimed to decipher full monologues in a garbled clip, or who insisted their recordings matched some buried fact about a location's past. If my experiment was any indication, most of them were correct less than twenty percent of the time. The rest? Just noise. Mistaken for meaning. And it wasn't dishonesty that fueled them—it was belief. Earnest, unshakable belief. But belief, no matter how deeply held, does not confer accuracy. Especially when the environment itself conspires to support the illusion.

We are extraordinarily good at convincing ourselves of nearly anything. Logic bends. Evidence wavers. And before long, we're defending the shape of our conclusions as though our lives depend on them. Planting flags in hills that may not even exist. And here's the hardest truth of all: *no one*—not even the skeptic—is immune.

That's the uncomfortable truth—the one most people, even seasoned investigators, don't want to admit. Intelligence doesn't shield you. Skepticism doesn't inoculate you. Experience doesn't guarantee immunity. Once emotion enters the frame, reason begins to blur.

A COOL AFTERNOON

I remember a case from the winter of 2014—a modest home in Lynn, Massachusetts. It was just me and a colleague. The homeowner, a quiet man who worked from home, had called us after noticing a pattern: every day around 3:30 in the afternoon, his office would grow cold. Not just in temperature, he said, but in feeling. The room changed. The air thickened. He described a weight, a creeping unease, as though something terrible was about to happen. He'd heard rumors— something about a death in that room years earlier—and the suggestion had taken root.

We arrived early, wanting to observe the full arc of the day. And just as he'd described, as the afternoon wore on, the room began to cool. Not metaphorically—literally. The temperature dropped. The homeowner grew visibly tense. The atmosphere felt charged, uncanny in its timing.

On the surface, it was compelling. A repeatable phenomenon. A single location. A consistent time. In paranormal research, those alignments are rare. But something felt off.

So I stepped back and did what I always tried to do first: eliminate the obvious. I checked the heating system. The thermostat. Vents. Airflow. No obvious issues. Then I looked more closely at the placement of the thermostat itself. It was mounted on an interior wall, just opposite a large window. And just above it, I noticed a sharp, angled shadow stretching across the casing—cast by the late-afternoon sun. That was the missing variable.

Each day, as the sun dipped westward, its rays passed through the window at the exact angle needed to strike the metal thermostat housing. The metal warmed, triggering a false temperature reading. The system, misled, shut off the heat. And just like that, the room cooled—right on time. Every afternoon. No ghosts. No presence. Just physics. A shadow, a sensor, and a perfect illusion. But for the man who lived there—who sat in that room every day, who'd heard whispers of a death, who felt the air change as the light fell—it wasn't just cold. It was *ominous*. The sensation wasn't just physical. It was emotional. And that emotion had meaning. It layered itself onto the data, coloring the experience until the two were indistinguishable.

That's how belief works. We interpret reality through more than facts. We bring fear. Nostalgia. Hope. We bring the aching human need for something to be *true*. And once a conclusion takes hold—especially one anchored in the personal—it becomes more than an idea. It becomes identity.

I've seen skilled investigators fall into that trap. Not because the evidence was compelling, but because the alternative was too barren. Too mechanical. Too unsatisfying. I've seen skeptics do the same—so determined to debunk that they refused to acknowledge anything unexplainable, even when it stared back at them. That's the wild card. The variable no meter can measure. Us.

Our brains are engines of pattern and inference. We fill gaps. We revise memory. We hear structure in static. And worse, we defend those illusions—sometimes fiercely— because to let them go would mean surrendering the story. And we're creatures of story, above all. Belief, in the end, is a form of survival. It gives the world shape. It imposes meaning. It keeps chaos at bay.

So when someone asks if I believe in ghosts, I pause. Because the answer depends on which kind they mean. The ones said to drift through bedrooms and basements? Or the ones that haunt our memory, our perception—our need for meaning? Either way, they're real. Just not always in the way we think.

CHAPTER NINE

ADDRESSING THE LIVING

One of the most unexpected outcomes of working in the paranormal wasn't what I discovered—it was who I discovered. Not spirits, but people. When I began this journey, I imagined the story would unfold through the data. I expected progress to come from invention, from field tests, from results. But time and again, it was the people I met who shaped the work. Some pushed me forward. Some dragged me sideways. A few, unfortunately, pulled me backward. But all of them—whether intentionally or not—left a mark.

Over the years, I worked with dozens of teams across multiple states, each with its own set of methods, rules, and beliefs. Some of them took the work seriously, even if their approach leaned more spiritual than scientific. Others were clearly in it for the spotlight. But a few—just a few—were doing something that resembled actual research. They asked real questions. They challenged each other. They kept their egos in check. And occasionally, they surprised me.

This chapter isn't a greatest-hits reel. It's not a list of characters or curiosities. It's a record of the human variable— the part of the process that couldn't be logged or measured but still influenced everything. Because every investigation was shaped by who was there, what they believed, and how they behaved when the lights went out. And if the search for the unknown teaches you anything, it's that people are far more unpredictable than phenomena.

Some of what I saw made me hopeful. Some of it frustrated me. But all of it taught me something—not just about the paranormal, but about belief, behavior, and the many ways people try to make sense of things they don't fully understand.

This chapter is about them. The ones who helped. The ones who hindered. And the ones I still think about.

WITCHES' INTEGRITY

If there was one thing that began to stand out to me as I worked with more and more teams, it was this: integrity wasn't universal. Some groups were searching for proof. Some were hunting for fame and attention. Some, whether they realized it or not, were simply high on the thrill of believing. But then there were the ones who impressed me for a very different reason—those who chased the truth, even when the truth was unsatisfying.

I found one of those rare groups in upstate New York. They called themselves Isis Investigations—Not *THAT* Isis, This was a coven of practicing witches who conducted their work with a method I hadn't seen before—and would never see again.

I first joined them for an investigation at the Knox Mansion in Johnstown, New York, a sprawling 19th-century estate with all the textbook ingredients of a haunting: family tragedy, decades of whispered stories, and the kind of heavy, quiet atmosphere that made you instinctively lower your voice when you walked through it.

Michael Baker and Patricia Gardner of
Isis Investigations.
Photo by Joanne Harritos 2006

From the start, Isis Investigations broke every convention I had grown used to. They didn't brief the team on the reported activity. They saved the Library for last, so no one would be influenced. They didn't need darkness. They didn't need midnight. They didn't even need a narrative. They conducted their investigation in broad daylight. They worked in total silence, walking alone through the mansion's many rooms, sometimes using pendulums or EM field meters, but always privately, quietly, deliberately.

No one compared notes. No one collaborated. For eight hours—yes eight hours, they worked like individual investigators solving their own cases, gathering impressions, feelings, and observations completely independent of each other. It wasn't until the very end, when we gathered in a meeting room at a nearby hotel, that they compared what they had found.

What shocked me wasn't just that they had uncovered many of the same hotspots and impressions without ever speaking to each other—it was what they told me next. When I asked them what evidence they had collected, their answer was simple and unwavering:

"We have none, we can't claim the place is haunted."

Not a single photograph. No recorded voices. No videos. No data that could be held up as proof. I pressed further.

"But, evidence aside, do you believe this place is haunted?"

Without hesitation, they all agreed.

"Oh yes. We believe this place is absolutely haunted."

And then came the sentence I will never forget.

"But belief isn't enough to present as evidence. We can't take a picture of a ghost and wrap it up in a box and hand it to you. It doesn't work that way. What we found here is personal. It's just something we can't prove."

In a field where so many people desperately wanted to validate their experiences, here was a group with the courage to say: *We believe, but we cannot prove*. That, to me, was the purest form of integrity I had ever seen in the paranormal community. It wasn't about convincing me, or the world. It was about being honest with themselves and the client.

I came to admire Isis Investigations deeply—not just for their process, but for their respect for the mystery and the truth. They didn't need to win an argument. They didn't need to "*catch*" a ghost on film. Their work was personal, sacred, and in many ways, humbling.

I stayed in touch with them long after the investigation. In fact, they later invited Joanne Harritos – my production team mate, and I to one of their Halloween ceremonies—a Samhain (*pronounced: 'Sow-en'*) celebration, marking the turning of the seasons and the thinning of the veil between worlds.

It was a private ritual, something few outsiders ever witnessed, and we were honored to be included. We stood in their circle, drank the libations, and listened as they chanted to the various powers of the universe—offering symbolic gifts to the goddess Isis, whose teachings guided their peaceful beliefs.

During those gatherings, we talked—not just about ghosts, but about life, nature, and the traditions that connected them to something larger. It was in these conversations that they told me about a ritual they performed called a Wiccaning. It's a sort of spiritual welcoming—a ceremony that introduces a child to the natural world and all of its elements. It wasn't a baptism. It wasn't a religious commitment. It was a simple but beautiful gesture—a way of saying, *you belong to this world, and you are part of it.*

Let me be clear: I'm an atheist. I'm a skeptic. I don't believe in the supernatural. But the idea of introducing my son to the world in this way struck me as meaningful—far more meaningful than many of the traditional religious ceremonies I'd seen.

It wasn't about pledging him to a faith—I would never do that. It was about introducing him to the earth, the air, the water, the sky—to life itself. And so, I chose to have my son blessed by the coven. To this day, I've never regretted that decision.

Isis Investigations left a lasting mark on me. Their process, their sincerity, and their honesty stayed with me throughout the rest of my journey. They showed me that not only is it possible to coexist with cultures vastly different from our own, but if peace is the mutual goal, it's also possible to genuinely respect the depth and care in one another.

In a field crowded with those eager to prove, to sell, to show—Isis Investigations quietly stood apart, and I never saw another group quite like them again.

HUMAN FIRST

Sometimes, it was kindness—the quiet kind that walks hand-in-hand with courage and restraint. There are moments in life that etch themselves into memory—not because of what was said, but because of how it was said.

Moments when someone's composure, someone's grace under pressure, rewires the entire room. I witnessed one of those moments at the Charlemont Inn in Charlemont, Massachusetts.

It was a joint investigation between two teams: the Spirit Encounter Research Team, or SERT, and New England Anomalies Research, commonly known as NEAR. NEAR was led by Keith and Sandra Johnson—veterans of the field and, as it turned out, familiar faces to anyone who had watched the early seasons of Ghost Hunters. Keith was a demonologist, and his twin brother, Carl, was as well. Both of them were soft-spoken, thoughtful, and approachable, despite their serious titles and heavy subject matter.

The night was chaotic from the start. During the setup, both teams were buzzing with activity—hauling in gear, chatting, laughing, testing walkie-talkies. The noise level crept higher and higher, until it apparently crossed a line for one of the inn's overnight guests.

The man came charging down the stairs, his face red, twisted with anger, his voice raised to a near-shout. He wasn't just frustrated by the noise—he was offended by the investigation itself. To him, our very presence was a violation of something sacred.

"You shouldn't be doing this!"

he barked, his fists clenched.

"You shouldn't be looking for spirits or demons! You're messing with things that aren't meant to be understood! That's for God to tell us—not you!"

Michael Baker, Rob Tremblay of *SERT* and
Keith Johnson of *NEAR*
Photo by Anthony Monti 2006

He began quoting scripture loudly, his voice shaking with rage, his body coiled as if he were preparing to unleash more. The air got heavy. Everyone stopped. For a moment, it felt like things could spiral. But that's when Keith stepped forward. No panic. No defensiveness. Just a calm smile. He approached the man slowly, like someone walking up to a frightened animal. And in the softest, most even tone, Keith said:

"I believe that."

Just those three words. It was like watching a balloon deflate. The man's fury melted almost instantly. His body relaxed. His face softened. It was as if someone had flipped a switch inside him.

Keith's calm, his kindness, his willingness to connect instead of confront—it disarmed the man in a way no argument ever could. Within minutes, they were chatting politely, as if the shouting match had never happened. The man eventually smiled, thanked Keith, and quietly returned to his room, his anger completely dissolved. Again, I'm not a religious person, and I don't subscribe to supernatural explanations. But what Keith did that night—that was something I never forgot.

It made me wonder if those who open themselves to spiritual spaces—believers or not—develop an emotional fluency the rest of us sometimes lack. Maybe they're better equipped to connect to the deeper, less accessible parts of other people. Or maybe Keith was just that rare kind of person—the kind who leads with kindness instead of ego. Either way, it stuck with me. In all my years filming ghost hunts, I saw plenty of people try to prove something. Very few ever proved themselves in the way Keith did that night.

THE AUTHORITY ILLUSION

In 2010, I traveled to Gettysburg, Pennsylvania, to attend a paranormal conference. It was the usual mix of lectures, vendor tables, and networking opportunities, and I was there to meet new people and maybe sell a few DVDs. At first, it felt like any other event. But then I saw someone I recognized—a name from the early days of my interest in the unexplained. And for a brief moment, I felt that old spark of curiosity flare back up.

This person had built a reputation as one of the so-called "*scientists of the paranormal.*" Years earlier, before I'd ever joined an investigative team or built my first device, this was exactly the kind of individual I imagined would dominate the field: *academically trained*, steeped in fringe science, and on the trail of answers that mainstream science ignored. According to his biography, he had worked on high-profile cases—some of which were adapted into major films—and had studied parapsychology at a California university back when such programs actually existed. It was, I thought, exactly what I'd always been looking for. But as they say, be careful what you wish for.

Out of caution and frankly a bit of legal concern, I won't name him here. He struck me as someone more than willing to protect his image through litigation. But I can say this much: once I met him, it didn't take long for the image to unravel.

At first, we got along. He liked my film, and I was excited to finally talk shop with someone I assumed was deeply credentialed and intellectually serious. But the longer we spoke, the more the cracks began to show. He was evasive about the actual details of his research, choosing instead to speak in vague, grandiose claims—always hinting at a breakthrough, but never offering anything concrete without a price tag. And the price was steep.

What he did talk about freely was other people—usually in a negative light. He was dismissive, arrogant, and openly misogynistic. It didn't take long for the awe to wear off. In time, I began to see that what I had mistaken for scientific authority was little more than theater. Even the few research methods he did describe were, in hindsight, thin on actual science. There's a lesson in that.

The paranormal field is full of self-declared experts—people who use inflated resumes, high investigation counts, and technical jargon to mask the absence of real evidence. You'll hear claims of 4,000 or 5,000 investigations, as if repetition itself is proof of ability.

But do the math. Four thousand cases spread across Thirty

years would require three to four investigations every week, without breaks, while also attending conventions and doing lectures. It just doesn't hold up.

Let's be clear: there are no experts in the paranormal. There is no standard, no certifying body, and most importantly, no proof. Anyone claiming authority over the unknown should be met with skepticism. Always.

THE CELEBRITY EXPERIMENT

In 2015, I was contacted by a man named George who was assembling a television pilot centered on the infamous Bridgewater Triangle—an area in southeastern Massachusetts long rumored to be a hotbed of unexplained activity. I don't recall exactly how he found my name, but somehow he did, and I was invited to be one of the featured investigators. Joe, my longtime colleague from Para-Boston, was brought on board as well.

The concept was straightforward: a small team would explore reports of strange phenomena throughout the triangle, combining history, folklore, and on-site investigation. But what gave the project a higher profile—and probably the funding—was its intended co-star: *Chris Jericho*. Yes, that *Chris Jericho*. World wrestling champion, front man of the band Fozzy, and, as it turns out, a genuine enthusiast of the paranormal.

Jericho, I learned, had been trying to develop a paranormal-themed series for years to complement his successful podcast. And to his credit, he wasn't just there for screen time. He was

Michael Baker and Chris Jericho during filming of *Unexplained America*
Photo by Joe Rainone 2016

grounded, curious, and genuinely interested in the subject. He asked thoughtful questions and seemed to understand the difference between entertainment and real investigation—something that couldn't be said for everyone on the production team.

My role was clear: I would be the science and tech guy, the one responsible for the experiments and the gear. One of the highlights for me was the opportunity to use a cesium vapor magnetometer—a high-end instrument typically reserved for geological surveys and archaeological digs.

It can detect disturbances in the Earth's magnetic field several feet below the surface, including remnants of old fire pits or metal artifacts. I had specifically requested it because part of our shoot involved the search for evidence of Native American activity. Burned wood, believe it or not, can hold magnetic signatures long after it cools.

It was shaping up to be the kind of project I had always hoped for: a serious exploration of paranormal claims with solid equipment and a broad audience. But then came the familiar tug of disappointment.

During filming, the producers began suggesting shortcuts. They wanted us to bury arrowheads in the ground, only to "*discover*" them on camera. It was supposed to create a more compelling moment for the network viewers who would decide the shows fate.

They weren't interested in waiting for legitimate results. They wanted excitement—now, guaranteed. I realize it was done in an effort to sell the show, but that moment said a lot. It reminded me, once again, that for most production companies, "*paranormal*" is just a genre. It's not a field of inquiry. It's a dramatic backdrop. And if reality doesn't cooperate, they'll script it until it does.

The pilot never made it to air, but it taught me a valuable lesson about how this industry works behind the curtain. Even with sincere people involved, the gravitational pull of entertainment usually wins. And unfortunately, the truth rarely survives the edit.

THE DEVIL AND THE DETAILS

In 2008, my team and I traveled to Clearwater, Florida, to attend TAPS CON—a large-scale paranormal convention organized around the popularity of the *Ghost Hunters* television series.

By that time, *14 Degrees* had been completed, and we were hoping the event would be a good place to sell DVDs, network with other investigators, and meet a few fans of the genre. But almost immediately, things didn't go to plan. Our shipment of DVDs was delayed.

The convention opened, and we had nothing to sell. So we improvised.

We converted our booth into a kind of pop-up interview

studio, inviting attendees to sit down and share their personal ghost stories on camera. It turned out to be a surprisingly effective move. Not only did we collect some fascinating material, but it gave us a unique opportunity to connect with people on a deeper level—hearing first-hand accounts from those who had come to the convention not just as fans, but as experiencers. Many of those stories would later find their way onto YouTube.

Midway through the event, I was hired to film a promotional piece for the following year's convention. That gig came with an all-access pass, which meant I was free to roam the venue, film panel discussions, and move among the guests and celebrities as I pleased.

It was a strange and memorable weekend, filled with appearances from SyFy Channel personalities, famous ghost hunters, and even a few unexpected names—like *Blue Öyster Cult*.

And then there was *Linda Blair*. The very one who gave the world one of the most iconic portrayals of demonic possession in cinematic history while playing Regan MacNeil in the Exorcist.

She was there to sign autographs and speak to fans, although I can't recall the subject of her talk. What I do remember—clearly—is a brief moment between her and *Keith Johnson*, a demonologist and one of the early contributors to *Ghost Hunters*. Keith approached her respectfully, introduced himself, and mentioned his role in the field. Linda paused. *"What's a demonologist?"* she asked.

It wasn't said with sarcasm or dismissal—just honest curiosity. But for me, standing nearby and witnessing the

Jason Hawes and Grant Wilson presenting.
Photo by Michael Baker 2011

exchange, it was a little surreal. Here was the actress whose iconic performance had shaped an entire generation's view of demons—and she had never even heard the word "*demonologist*." Of course, she's an actor, not a theologian or an investigator. No one should expect her to be an expert in the field just because she played a role. But the moment was telling. It underscored just how wide the gulf really is between Hollywood's version of the paranormal and the real-world community of researchers, believers, and skeptics.

It was a reminder that what we see on screen—whether in movies or reality TV—is rarely more than performance. And yet, that performance shapes public understanding far more than any genuine investigation ever will.

TAPS AND KNOCKS

It would be impossible to reflect on my time in the paranormal field without mentioning the group that helped launch the modern ghost-hunting phenomenon: The Atlantic Paranormal Society, better known as TAPS.

The influence of TAPS—and by extension, *Ghost Hunters*, the television series that made them a household name—was undeniable. They were the face of 21st-century paranormal investigation, and the standard-bearers for countless teams that would follow. It's no exaggeration to say that the popularity of ghost hunting as a hobby, as a genre, and even as an industry, can be traced back to them.

I think it fair to note that the convention I mentioned earlier—TAPS CON—bore their name, but not their imprint. Despite the branding, the event wasn't organized or funded by the TAPS team themselves. It was the brainchild of an independent promoter, hoping to capitalize on the group's fame, and ultimately ended up in some hot water as a result. TAPS was merely the draw, not the organizer.

Over my thirteen years of work in the field, I had the chance to meet—and in some cases, work alongside—every major cast member of the show. I even conducted a few investigations with Adam Berry before he was selected to join the series. And while every encounter was cordial, one thing always stood out to me: a marked difference in demeanor between the long-time veterans of the show and those who had been brought in later. The originals—Jason, Grant, Steve— carried themselves with a kind of emotional fatigue. Not disinterest, exactly, but a wariness. As though years of scrutiny, fan attention, and behind-the-scenes politics had taken their toll. They were polite, friendly even. But careful.

Conversations with them always felt a bit rehearsed—like every word had been vetted through the filter of a non-disclosure agreement. And perhaps it had.

I remember filming a promotional video at TAPS CON, making the rounds to collect quick "*See you next year*" sound bites from the cast. When I approached Steve Gonsalves, he politely declined. He explained that he hadn't signed a contract for the next year's event and didn't want to misrepresent anything on camera. It struck me as an honorable stance—and a telling one.

At after-parties and social events, I spent time with Brian Harnois, one of the original cast members from the early seasons. Brian had become something of a lightning rod— portrayed on the show as the high-strung skeptic, and later vilified as unreliable or unstable. But in person, he was kind, thoughtful, and, frankly, a bit overwhelmed by the spotlight. The show had laid bare some of his personal struggles, framing them for dramatic effect. It felt like a cheap ratings ploy. What made it worse was discovering that, in the early years, not everyone on the show was paid. Jason and Grant were compensated. Steve eventually was. But Brian, despite being broadcast to millions each week—despite being at the center of the drama—wasn't on the payroll (at least initially as far as I know). Unfortunately that's how media works: not always fair, rarely kind, and often indifferent to the people it uses for content.

For all the ghost stories told under red lights and in hushed voices, the real performance has always taken place off camera—at the booths, behind the autograph tables, and in the hotel bars after convention hours. If the early 2000s marked the rise of the televised ghost hunter, the years that followed gave birth to an entire ecosystem of personalities, personas, and brands. Some were sincere. Some were savvy. A few were just there for the photo ops.

Over time, I began to realize that the paranormal world—at least the public-facing one—had more in common with professional wrestling than it did with science. That wasn't a slight, just an observation. There were faces and heels, hype and backstories, signature moves and catchphrases. There were even scripted tensions, exaggerated for dramatic effect and replayed from city to city. If you had the right charisma, the right buzzwords, and enough willingness to blur the line between performance and belief, you could make a living playing the part of an expert.

But behind the curtain, the mood was different. TAPS, for example, helped ignite the ghost hunting boom, yet most of its members appeared weary, even guarded, when approached. Not unfriendly—just understandably cautious, like people who'd had too many strangers mistake them for something they weren't. Their public image had been molded by editors and contracts. The real people behind those faces seemed… quieter. More complex. Maybe even a little disillusioned.

Others, like the so-called scientist I met in Gettysburg, were something else entirely. He had the suit, the backstory, the vague claims of revolutionary discoveries—but no substance behind the curtain. He was the wizard behind the smoke machine, only without the magic. Yet people followed him. Quoted him. Paid him. That's the power of authority, even when it's self-appointed.

Then there were moments of friction between belief and branding—like when the producers of our TV pilot asked us to fake evidence, or when Linda Blair, so iconic in horror history, seemed bewildered at the idea of a real demonologist. The lines between pop culture and actual research, between entertainment and inquiry, were so thoroughly blurred that even the people at the center of it seemed unsure where one ended and the other began.

And that's what this chapter was really about: not just the people, but the roles they played. Some performed them knowingly. Others were pulled into them. A few resisted the script entirely. It's easy to forget, especially when the lights are bright and the crowds are loud, that none of this has ever really been about ghosts. It's been about belief—how it's sold, how it's staged, and how it survives in the echo of applause.

In the end, television didn't just change the paranormal. It packaged it. And if you looked closely, the real haunting wasn't on screen. It was in the faces of the people trying to live up to the part.

CHAPTER TEN

THE LONG GOODBYE

By the end of 2016, something had shifted. I wasn't chasing new experiments or designing gear. I was looking backward. It had been over a decade since we shot *14 Degrees*. That number felt strange—impossible, almost. Ten years since those long, winding drives to unfamiliar towns, the bleary-eyed editing marathons, the weekends that vanished into basements and back roads. A few years earlier, I stopped pressing new DVDs. I figured if anyone was still curious, they'd find it. So I uploaded it to YouTube. For free. I didn't expect much. But within two years, it had passed two million views. It was humbling. And, I'll admit, kind of cool. Not long after, I was talking to Joe Rainone—a friend and Para-Boston colleague. Joe had a way of spotting potential where others saw closure. With the 10-year anniversary of the film's release approaching in 2017, he floated an idea that stopped me cold: What if we went back? Revisit the people we interviewed. Ask the same questions. See what changed.

From a research standpoint, it struck me hard. A decade-later follow-up like that is rare in this field. Belief, after all, is slippery—especially when filtered through time. The scope felt massive. But I said yes.

I started reaching out. Some people were hard to find. Some politely declined. But others welcomed the idea—genuinely happy to reconnect and reflect. For many of them, the original film had marked a strange, meaningful chapter in their lives. Some had stepped away from the field entirely. Others remained involved in quieter ways. But all of them, without exception, had been changed by the experience.

I reassembled the old *New Gravity Media* crew—Anthony Monti and Joanne Harritos—and now with Joe in the mix, the four of us set out again. But this time, we weren't chasing phenomena. We were chasing people.

Nearly everyone from the original film agreed to sit down with us again. Some were well-known. Others had only appeared briefly. But each had helped shape the story the first time around, and meeting them again felt like flipping through a photo album where the faces had aged but the memories hadn't.

Rick Boisvere, the psychic medium, was still thoughtful and grounded—his presence unchanged. He hadn't abandoned his beliefs, but his view of the field had evolved. The excitement, he said, had dulled. The community felt thinner now. He wasn't bitter—just more observant.

Final interview with psychic medium Rick Boisvere for the filming of
14 Degrees - Revisited. 2017

Josh Mantello, who used to spend weekends chasing shadows through Houghton Mansion in North Adams, Massachusetts, now found clarity in hiking the Berkshires. He spoke with a kind of peace I didn't remember from before. Like someone who'd finally stopped holding his breath

And Steve Gonsalves? Still immersed, still evolving. He talked candidly about production shifts and methodology, about the machinery behind modern paranormal media. Back when I first interviewed him, the TAPS team's ten-year contract with the SyFy Channel had just begun. Now, it was ending. Despite everything, he sounded calm. Grounded. Ready for whatever came next. He even hinted at a new project—something he couldn't talk about yet. I still wonder what it was.

No one interview stood out as *the* moment. There was no dramatic arc. But there was something honest in the quiet repetition of it all. We weren't documenting belief anymore. We were documenting what belief becomes. There were others

Final interview with Steve Gonsalves of *TAPS/Ghost Hunters* for the filming of
14 Degrees - Revisited. 2017

I had hoped to revisit. Threads I wanted to pull. Footage I
imagined capturing. At one point, I had a list: ideas, locations,
reflections I thought would bring it all full circle. But
somewhere along the way—quietly, steadily—the drive to
finish it drained out of me. Not in a dramatic flash. More like
a slow leak—like a balloon gradually losing air. I found
myself staring at timelines and rough cuts, asking, *"What am
I really trying to say here?"*

The editing, the promotion, the funding—it all weighed on
me like a 300lb stone I had no chance of moving. And no one
else on the team wanted to carry it either. Not even Joe, who
had sparked the idea in the first place. At the time, my son was
three. My wife and I had just bought a fixer-upper, and every
free hour was swallowed by remodeling. I still had my day job,
too. The bandwidth simply wasn't there—not mentally,

emotionally, or practically.

So the project faded. Quietly. Without ceremony. And when I stepped back and really examined the question—what was I hoping to convey?—I wasn't sure I had an answer that mattered to anyone but me. The idea had been to check in. To see where people landed. But would that resonate with the millions who'd watched *14 Degrees*? Or was it just me trying to make sense of something I hadn't quite let go of?

After filming the majority of return interviews, it felt less like a documentary and more like a reunion. We weren't chasing phenomena anymore—we were debriefing a shared event. Like survivors of some strange expedition, comparing notes years later. There were good stories in those

Final interview with Brian Jenkins and Terri D'Amico for the filming of *14 Degrees - Revisited*. 2017

conversations. Honest ones. But they were personal. And I realized the film had never been popular enough to carry that kind of nostalgia to strangers.

It felt like going back to a town you used to live in. The

Final interview with Patricia Gardner and Setheesh Vijayan of Isis Investigations for
the filming of *14 Degrees - Revisited*. 2017

streets are familiar, but some buildings are gone. Trees you
remember have been cut down. Others have grown in their
place. There's life, still—just different than before. It's not
better or worse. Just changed. And while you might be
tempted to think your time there was the golden age, there's a
whole generation now who sees it differently. For them, this is
the golden age.

That's what it felt like revisiting the paranormal field from
a decade earlier. People from the early 2000s had either moved
on or adapted. And like any field that evolves, sometimes the
biggest revelation is that the mystery you were chasing…
might not have been there to begin with. Sometimes the real
discovery isn't what you found. It's what you let go of. But
this departure wasn't the final moment of the slow exile I'd
begun. It may have marked the end of my interest in film
production, but the research—the real work—was still alive,
at least for a while.

I continued meeting with Para-Boston. I still joined

investigations. And yes, I was still unpacking my homemade contraptions, setting up sensors, and trying to capture some tangible, measurable element of the paranormal experience. But looking back, even those efforts had become more reflective than exploratory. And if there's one thing I've learned about myself, it's that when I start looking backward more than forward, something inside me is already letting go.

The reasons for that slow withdrawal weren't singular. They built up over time. Layer upon layer. So I'll do my best to explain. First, there were the people. Not the ones I specifically worked beside. Not the sincere investigators quietly chipping away at the unknown. I'm talking about the crowds—the masses that flooded conventions, clutching glossy photos, lining up for autographs, cheering for their favorite television ghost hunters like they were rock stars. The energy was infectious, yes—but it was misplaced. Misguided. I'd stood on those stages, too. Spoken before packed halls at major conventions like *Dragon Con*. Presented research to rooms filled with investigators, team leaders, weekend hobbyists, and curious onlookers.

I'd laid out new concepts—methodologies rooted in cognitive science, technology, and experimental design. I made the case for a shift in how we approached this work. But no matter how well the ideas were received in the moment, they rarely stuck. Instead, people clung to the same old practices—dowsing rods, flashlight tricks, Spirit Boxes spitting out garbled nonsense—all popularized by television and repeated endlessly by teams hoping to mimic what they saw on screen. It didn't seem to matter how many times we demonstrated the flaws in those methods. They had momentum. Familiarity. And most importantly, they had spectacle. You can't compete with spectacle. Not easily.

The television networks had long arms reaching deep into the culture and shaping how belief was packaged and sold. Their influence seeped into every corner of the field, setting the standard for what "*investigation*" was supposed to look like. And no matter how sincere someone's intentions might have been, most people eventually conformed to the script. They wanted to believe. And they wanted others to see them believing. It was frustrating—not because people believed differently than I did, but because they weren't really thinking critically at all. They weren't just believing—they were performing belief.

Over time, I felt like I was speaking a different language— one that fewer and fewer people were interested in learning. And the more I watched the same tired methods being celebrated as breakthroughs, the more isolated I felt in my own work. I wasn't angry. Just tired. Because belief is easy. But inquiry is hard. And trying to push for meaningful change in a space that's built on emotional reinforcement… that's exhausting.

THE RECKONING

Over the course of the following year, I found myself drawn back—not to the investigations or the equipment, but to the quiet aftermath. The dust had settled, and what remained was the question I'd avoided asking: Had it all meant something? I wasn't searching for proof anymore. I was looking for thread—something that could bind thirteen years of effort into a shape that felt coherent. Purposeful. Worth the cost.

There were indeed moments that lingered. I made friends, of course—and a few adversaries, too. That's inevitable when you spend long nights in the

Maine PRI-ME kidding around during an investigation.

dark with people, waiting for silence to give up its secrets. Bonds form quickly in that space, stitched together by boredom, adrenaline, and shared hope. Some moments from those years still make me laugh, especially in hindsight. During one investigation, I managed—entirely by accident—to turn off a lighthouse. A real lighthouse. The Coast Guard showed up minutes later, banging on the door, demanding an explanation I wasn't quite prepared to give.

At a library investigation, I forgot that most modern smoke detectors are ion-based—something I should have remembered before firing up a Van de Graaff generator. We were midway through a session when the alarms screamed to life, and within minutes, the fire department was standing in the foyer looking thoroughly unconvinced.

Another time, while presenting at a convention, my Tesla coil took out the DJ's laptop mid-set. It wasn't funny then—but it is now. These were the chaotic, oddly charming detours of the journey—moments that didn't advance the work, but made it human. But then there were the achievements. Not the kind that make headlines or win awards—but the quieter kind, earned slowly, deliberately. The kind that only matter if you care about the work.

PURPOSE AND ACCOMPLISHMENT

I brought structure to a domain ruled by hunches. Where others leaned on intuition and folklore, I introduced process. Systems. I designed tools that could parse signal from noise, isolate variables, and capture slow environmental drift—the kinds of changes no one thought to measure. While teams chased chills and shadows, I was logging data. Plotting spectrograms. Calibrating instruments to test claims that had only ever been felt, not measured.

Where others listened, I recorded. Where they speculated, I traced. I turned vague impressions into testable events—into patterns that could be tracked, questioned, repeated. A circuit

First field experiment at
The Colonial House Inn. 2008

board was as much a compass to me as any EM field detector. I brought the discipline of an engineer into rooms clouded by anecdote, and I made uncertainty quantifiable.

There were moments that resisted explanation—recordings that surfaced on hardware never meant to capture sound, geological alignments that echoed local legend a little too precisely. Anomalies emerged, persistent and defiant. But I didn't frame them as answers. I treated them as questions—questions that demanded better tools, sharper methods, and more than thirty experimental devices to even begin to understand.

I spoke at conferences. Published findings. Pulled back the curtain on the plastic theatrics of ghost-hunting gadgets—devices built more for drama than discovery. I made a documentary. I developed pitches. I stood on stages before audiences who

Investigating the *Connors Farm* in Beverly, MA where mysterious drumming was recorded on a coil mic prototype. 2016

wanted wonder, not scrutiny. Who wanted confirmation, not control conditions.

I didn't just chase anomalies. I pursued accountability. And in the process, I learned something that had nothing to do with spirits or electromagnetic fields. I learned about people. Most aren't looking for truth. They're looking for belief. Not all. But enough. Enough to shape the narrative, influence the culture, and crowd out any competing signal. Because belief comforts. It affirms. It gives you a story that ends neatly—often in a place you already hoped it would.

Truth, by contrast, demands discomfort. It requires humility. It's slower, quieter, and far less generous to the ego. And in a field built around wonder and dread, truth loses that contest almost every time.

Over the years, I came to recognize a pattern: the illusion of inquiry masking a longing for affirmation. People weren't testing ideas. They were enacting them—performing curiosity while quietly praying for the outcome they'd already chosen. That's not research. That's theatre.

THE DRIFT

After all that time, I'm left with only a few moments I can't explain. A short list. A handful, at most. And yet, I never saw the years as wasted. Because what mattered wasn't the mystery—it was the method.

Pilot of web show *Mystery Lab* where science principles, helpful in paranormal research, were demonstrated on air. 2008

I gave every theory its day in court. Scientific or spiritual, conventional or fringe—I treated them all the same: tested, repeated, observed. I didn't stage results. I didn't cut around the quiet moments to build a narrative. In my films, I let people tell their stories in their own words—no voice-over steering the viewer toward awe or doubt. If the silence was real, I left it in. What I found was rarely cinematic. But it was honest.

I began to think of it like gold panning. Most days, you sift through silt and come up empty. But once in a while, something glints. Something real. And that glint—however rare—keeps you looking. If your goal is applause, you give up. But if you're after understanding, you stay with the river.

Most of the teams I met were simply chasing an experience. A way to slip outside the mundane. That's not a criticism, necessarily. There's comfort in mystery that facts can't replicate. But for me, belief alone was never enough. I wanted to know.

As an engineer, I was wired to break things down—to question assumptions, test boundaries, analyze failure points. I applied that same mindset to the unknown. Before I could accept an idea, I had to stress test it. Turn it over. Measure its weight. I didn't force it to fit if it didn't. And when something failed the test, I let it go. To someone watching from the outside, it might have looked like failure. Thirteen years. Dozens of prototypes. Hundreds of hours. And still, no proof. No smoking gun. Nothing that might shift the cultural needle. But I never defined success by the size of the claim. Because here's what I did find: there is something. Rare. Elusive. Occasionally observable—but not easily defined. I can't tell you what it is. I won't pretend it's a spirit, or an energy, or the residue of trauma echoing through space.

Maybe it's environmental. Maybe it's psychological. Maybe it's something else entirely. But it moves people. It plants stories. It changes the air in a room. And whatever that is, it's worth examining. What made the pursuit difficult wasn't just the evasiveness of the phenomena. It was everything that surrounded it—the noise, the show, the ever-churning engine of performance.

For every measured conversation, there were ten more brimming with ego. For every team grounded in reason, a dozen more were chasing camera time. The culture was thick with theatrics masquerading as science—people wielding equipment like talismans, reciting jargon they didn't understand, creating tension where none existed. And through it all, the real work—the honest, careful, methodical effort—was slowly being drowned out.

Then there were the people at the center of it all—the clients. Some were sincere, others skeptical. A few were wounded, and more than a few were simply hoping to be part of a story. Often, what they described wasn't supernatural at all. It was grief. It was loneliness. It was trauma reaching for form. The line between experience and interpretation was rarely clear, and parsing it required not just skepticism, but compassion. That tightrope—between empathy and evidence—wore thin.

LETTING GO

When I first stepped into this field, the refrain was always the same: *we're here to help people.* Nearly every investigator I met echoed it, sometimes with conviction, sometimes with the hollow certainty of something repeated too often to be questioned. I didn't always believe it—not entirely. But as motives go, it wasn't the worst one to claim.

Back then, the people reaching out to us felt different too—less filtered, less performative. There was an emotional rawness to their stories, a kind of vulnerability that hadn't yet been flattened by reality TV tropes or social media theatrics. Maybe that was before the full weight of cultural spectacle settled over the field—before the investigations themselves became a kind of entertainment.

One woman—I'll call her Marianne—contacted us a few months after her husband passed. She wasn't distraught. She wasn't hoping for cameras or cold spots or closure packaged in infrared. She was simply unmoored.

She said the house had changed in a way she couldn't quite articulate. It wasn't silent, exactly. Just… displaced. The normal creaks and sighs of a settling home now felt misaligned, as though the walls themselves were adjusting to the absence. Shadows moved where they shouldn't, though never in a way that frightened her. It wasn't fear she felt—it was sorrow.

When we arrived, she didn't usher us in like a hostess preparing for a show. There were no guests, no dimmed lights, no hushed excitement. She brewed tea. She sat with us, and she talked.

We went through the motions—unpacked the gear, ran the cables, set up the recorders. But it quickly became clear that none of it mattered. Not really. Marianne wasn't asking for evidence. She was asking for understanding. For someone to tell her that the strange quiet of her home wasn't all in her head. That maybe absence could take shape. That maybe grief could echo.

We spent most of the night listening. She told us about his laugh. The way he fixed the screen door every spring, unprompted. How the silence now didn't feel peaceful—it felt fractured. There were no voices caught on tape. No temperature shifts. No shadows. Just memories. And in that moment, it was enough. Before we left, she said something I still remember:

"I don't need you to find him. I just didn't want to feel crazy
for thinking he might still be here."

There was nothing to document, no scene to include in a reel. But it remains one of the few investigations that felt complete—not because of what we discovered, but because nothing needed discovering. We just needed to be there, and maybe that's what made the later cases so difficult to reconcile. The shift was stark. The meaning, harder to find.

In those final years, something subtle—but telling—began to shift in the cases we were called to. The urgency was gone. Fear had been replaced by fascination, and sincerity gave way to performance.

More and more, clients didn't seem to want resolution—they wanted a show. It became common to arrive at a home and find guests already gathered, wine glasses in hand, waiting for the spooky entertainment to begin.

I remember one case vividly: a woman who'd reported footsteps, shadows, the sense of being watched. But the moment we arrived, she was practically buzzing with excitement, hurrying us to set up, dim the lights, and let the *"real"* part of the night begin. At one point, she streamed the DVR monitor feed to Facebook Live, narrating it like a ghost-hunting influencer. This wasn't someone seeking answers. This was someone hosting an event.

I'll be the first to admit that by then, my patience had worn thin. It's possible my reading of these encounters was colored by fatigue, or a quiet bitterness I hadn't yet acknowledged. But something had changed. In one house, conflicting stories from family members unraveled the moment we asked a few basic questions. In another, friends had been invited to "*watch the ghost hunt.*" One person joked that she hoped we caught something, "*so we'd come back for a Part Two.*" These weren't outliers. They were becoming the norm. And as this shift took hold, I began to wonder about the people who didn't call. The ones who might have been afraid, confused, or grieving—but who kept quiet because the culture around hauntings had turned performative. Because the circus that followed a team's arrival made them feel foolish for even asking. It's hard to know how many voices went silent while everyone else played pretend.

Eventually, I had to acknowledge a shift I didn't want to see. The climb was no longer upward. The ground itself had started to erode. I wasn't gaining traction. The foundation I had spent years trying to build—a space for restraint, for clarity, for open but honest inquiry—had no place to take root. Not in the spotlight. Not in the noise.

The audience I thought I was reaching didn't want what I was offering. They didn't want nuance. They wanted certainty. They didn't want careful questioning. They wanted affirmations. They didn't want science. They wanted a carnival. And the more I tried to bring reason into the conversation, the more distant it felt. Not because people couldn't follow, but because they weren't interested in following. Their stories were already written. Mine simply didn't match.

At times, it felt like a years-long standoff with the most devout believers. Not just disagreement, but outright resistance—emotional, defensive, often hostile. There were moments when I felt like the only adult in the room, gently trying to explain that Santa Claus wasn't real. And more often than not, I was treated accordingly.

What I came to understand is this: being wrong is uncomfortable, yes—but being fooled by your own senses, your own certainty, cuts deeper. It brushes too close to something more fragile—our grip on reality, our sense of trust in ourselves. Maybe that's why some held on so tightly. Admitting error was one thing. But admitting misperception? That felt, to many, like stepping toward madness. I don't say that with judgment. I say it because I saw it—over and over again.

I spent more than a decade trying to build a bridge between skepticism and wonder. But each time I laid a plank, it cracked beneath the pressure—under the weight of expectation, fandom, and the seductive draw of certainty. The bridge didn't break all at once. It just stopped holding. So I did the only thing I could. I stepped away.

Not with a dramatic exit or a closing statement. Just... gradually. Fewer meetings. Fewer investigations. Less time spent explaining what made sense only in the gray. I turned toward other parts of life—my family, my career, and the quieter questions that didn't need proving. I never stopped being curious. But I stopped trying to prove something to people who weren't listening.

It wasn't defeat. It was release. Like setting down a pack you've carried for too long. The need to justify. To defend. To explain. That weight accumulates, and when the return is so small, letting go becomes a kind of clarity. No regrets.

I built things no one else had. I asked questions most people avoided. I caught a few fleeting moments that still make me wonder. I met people who changed my view, challenged my assumptions, and reminded me why I began this work at all. That kind of search—one guided not by belief, but by the hunger to understand—is rare, and it's worth something.

If I left anything behind in this field, I hope it's this: a quiet reminder that mystery deserves better than performance. That belief and inquiry are not the same. That "*I don't know*" can be the most honest thing we say—and that truth, however small, is always enough.

CHAPTER ELEVEN

REMAINS OF THE DAY

They say hindsight is 20/20—but clarity after the fact isn't the same as wisdom. Of course things make sense in retrospect—once you've failed enough times, the path forward always looks clearer. But that doesn't mean your second guesses would've been right either. Hindsight might sharpen the view, but it doesn't guarantee the truth. It just makes the missteps easier to catalog.

Over the last thirteen years, there were plenty of things I did that didn't pan out. Projects that stalled, partnerships that fell apart, ideas that never quite lived up to their promise. And yes, I crossed paths with more than a few con artists—people who wore conviction like a costume, selling certainty to anyone willing to listen. If I told you I didn't regret the time I spent with some of them, I'd be lying. But when it comes to the research itself, I have no regrets. Not a single one.

Every result—positive, negative, or inconclusive—was still a result. Even silence carries meaning if you're paying attention. And when your goal is to uncover the truth, you have to be ready for whatever shape it takes. Sometimes that shape is unremarkable. Sometimes it's inconvenient. But it's still the truth. The only failure is refusing to recognize it when it shows up.

People ask me now and then what I'd be doing if I hadn't stepped away. What experiments I would've kept pursuing. What questions I'd still be asking. It's not an easy thing to answer. Most of what I was already working on came down to just two variables: time and money. But of the two, time is the one you never get back. You can always earn more money. You can't buy another year.

Several of my devices showed promise—real potential. They just needed to run longer, in the right places, under the right conditions. That's the catch with data: it's not always about what you build. Sometimes, it's just about giving something enough time to catch what the rest of us miss.

But time is a luxury. If you want a normal life, with a job and a family and some semblance of stability, you're already working at a deficit. That's why I tried to encourage others to pick up where I left off.

I believed—and still do—that if enough curious minds came together, if enough people cared to look, we might actually discover something that lasts. But belief is a closed loop for many.

People who are convinced they've already found the answer rarely go searching for another one. So what about the paths I never got to explore? Where would I have gone if I'd had more time, more resources, or just a longer fuse? That's an even harder question.

The physical world is vast. You could spend a lifetime chasing the edge of a single theory in quantum mechanics or psychology and still leave most of it untouched. I don't consider myself particularly special—I've led an ordinary life, with an ordinary set of skills. But I had one advantage: I stayed curious and determined. That's all you really need. Curiosity, commitment, and the patience to wait for an answer that might take years to arrive.

PRIMARY PERCEPTIONS

One area I always meant to explore more deeply—maybe even obsessively—was the work of Cleve Backster. Backster was a polygraph examiner in the 1960s, known for a moment that would've seemed absurd if it hadn't changed the course of his life. One day, standing in his office, he watered his dracaena plant and wondered—half out of boredom, half out of curiosity—how long it would take the water to reach the leaves.

He hooked up his polygraph electrodes to the leaf and waited. What he saw surprised him. An electrical reaction similar to galvanic skin responses. Later, just to see what would happen, he considered burning one of the plant's leaves to elicit a reaction. But before he could act—before he even struck the match or made any movement at all—the plant's electrical signal spiked.

It was as if it sensed his intent. That one response launched decades of experiments—not just with plants, but with living foods, bacteria, and even isolated human cells.

Backster spent the rest of his life trying to understand that signal, chasing the idea that intention itself could be measured, and that life—at every level—might be listening.

The scientific community sharply criticized Backster's work—largely because his findings were never peer-reviewed, and the results were said to be inconsistent at best.

He published his theories in a book titled *Primary Perception*, and continued developing his experiments for the rest of his life. But like many researchers operating on the fringe, Backster eventually fell into a familiar trap: designing experiments to confirm his hypothesis, rather than challenge it. That's where real inquiry ends and pseudoscience begins.

Still, I couldn't shake the feeling that there might have been something there—some kernel of truth buried beneath the flaws in his method. I didn't buy the conclusions, necessarily, but I believed the questions were worth asking.

After all, modern science has since shown that plants engage in complex chemical signaling, and can detect and respond to environmental changes. They can even share information through root systems. None of that proves consciousness. But it proves interaction—and interaction is measurable.

I remember when *MythBusters* tackled Backster's theory.

They designed an episode around the idea that plants might respond to harm done nearby, attempting to recreate Backster's methods with their own brand of experimental rigor. For most of the segment, they actually recorded positive results—minor fluctuations that seemed to support his claims. But in the final test, they declared the theory "*busted*," and every time I re-watch it, I find myself rolling my eyes.

The critical final experiment involved Grant Imahara dropping a carton of eggs into a pot of boiling water, hoping the nearby plant would register a stress response. When no reaction occurred, they called the hypothesis dead. But here's the problem: *they used store-bought eggs.*

Backster had emphasized—repeatedly—that his results only occurred with living cells. Commercial eggs are pasteurized and homogenized. In many cases, they're infertile, processed, and biologically inert.

Whatever potential signal might have existed was already long gone. To me, that misstep undermined the whole experiment. It was like trying to measure heart rate on a mannequin. That's not to say Backster was right. But if you're going to test an idea, you have to meet it on its own terms. Otherwise, you're not investigating—you're just performing dismissal.

Funny enough, I did dip a toe into this line of inquiry— once or twice, at least. Around 2013, my focus had shifted toward measuring physiological reactions in people during alleged paranormal events. I was interested in what the body might reveal that the mind couldn't yet explain. So I built a simple galvanic skin response (GSR) meter—a tool commonly used in polygraph exams to detect minute changes in perspiration, which correlate with stress or arousal.

I had other devices too—ones that measured heart rate, temperature, and other biometric data. Taken together, they formed the rough outline of a portable polygraph system. But that's a story for another time.

During an investigation at a private residence in Lynn, Massachusetts, I decided—on a whim—to try something different. I attached the GSR leads not to a person, but to a plant in the living room. It was a basic Pothos, if I recall correctly. I left the sensor in place and let it run for most of the night, logging the data quietly in the background while the main investigation unfolded, and, to my surprise, I did get a few spikes in the data.

Small, erratic jumps in conductivity—momentary reactions that suggested something had changed. But I couldn't correlate them with anything happening in the room. No corresponding movement. No temperature shifts. No audio cues. It was just noise—interesting, but inconclusive.

The truth is, that experiment wasn't the focus of the investigation. It was something I set up on the side, half out of curiosity and half in homage to Backster's work. Still, that Pothos experiment lingers in my mind—not as proof, but as potential. I wonder what I might have seen if I'd approached it more deliberately.

ELECTRIC FIELDS

If time and money weren't such unforgiving constraints,

there's one project I would have loved to see through to completion: a grid-based electric field sensor array I began researching in early 2017, just before I started to quietly step away from the field. It was one of those ideas that seemed almost too elegant to ignore.

The premise was rooted in a simple analogy. Imagine a room not as empty space, but as a container—like a fish tank. And instead of water, it's filled with electrons, ambient energy distributed evenly throughout the environment. Now drop an object into that tank—say, an orange—and you can measure its presence by the volume of water it displaces. If electrons behave similarly, then an object entering the room should theoretically disturb the field in a measurable way. The key was to find a way to detect that displacement and translate it into usable data.

That was the vision: to detect the presence of something not by seeing it, or hearing it, but by measuring the invisible ripple it left behind. Initially, I thought I could build a single device to capture that displacement across a broad area. But the reality proved far more difficult. The precision required to measure such subtle fluctuations across an entire room exceeded the capability of any one sensor. I needed a new approach—something modular, distributed, scalable.

That's when I discovered the Plessey EPIC sensor—an integrated circuit developed for medical applications. It was designed to pick up the minute electrical fluctuations caused by the beating of a human heart. In clinical settings, it was used to measure bioelectric signals without direct contact— just proximity to the body's natural field.

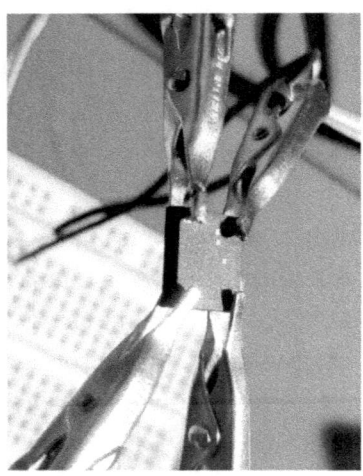

Plessey Sensor IC connected for testing. Clamps were used to prevent over heating.

It was a breakthrough. If the sensor could detect a heartbeat, perhaps it could also detect other disturbances in the electric field. I began to imagine a grid of these sensors—dozens, arranged across a space, each one monitoring a small radius. With the right amplification and custom software, I could triangulate the location, size, and movement of anything passing through the grid. It would be the closest thing to building a digital net for invisible energy.

The concept was promising enough to catch the attention of television producer Seanbaker Carter, who offered early support and funding. I purchased five of the sensors myself and built a basic prototype. But despite the promise, the range was disappointing—barely a foot, even with amplification. Far short of the three or four feet I had hoped for.

To make matters worse, the sensors were extraordinarily delicate. Sensitive to current, vulnerable to static discharge. I burned through four during testing. Seanbaker generously ordered more, but even after consulting directly with the manufacturer, I couldn't improve the range. And as the price of the chips climbed, continuing the project became harder to justify. Eventually, I had to shelve it.

I still think about that sensor grid—what it might have revealed with more time and a proper lab. It's one of the few projects I walked away from reluctantly. Unfortunately, I just couldn't afford to keep chasing it. But that's the thing about unfinished work—it doesn't vanish. It just waits, quietly.

Michael Baker speaking about the electric field location experiment. 2017

ENVIRONMENTAL INFLUENCE

If I'd had the opportunity to launch a full-scale study, one that required time, funding, and academic support, I would've focused on a question that's quietly haunted my work for years: how much of what we interpret as paranormal is actually a response to the environment itself?

I'm not talking about EM field meters or gadgets that chirp when you hold them near a power strip. I mean real environmental influence—measurable, pervasive forces like infrasound, geomagnetic variation, barometric pressure, or ion concentrations in the air. Factors that are often overlooked because they don't lend themselves to a show. They don't beep or blink. They don't make for good TV. But they might be shaping our perception more than anyone realizes.

Infrasound, for instance—low-frequency sound below the range of human hearing—has been linked in some studies to feelings of anxiety, unease, and even the sensation of a "*presence*" in the room.

These aren't theories born from ghost stories; they're

conclusions drawn from controlled experiments in sound labs and architectural acoustics. A room with the wrong kind of resonance can, quite literally, make people feel haunted.

Then there are geomagnetic fields. Earth's magnetic field isn't a static shell—it fluctuates constantly in response to solar storms, subterranean shifts, and even regional anomalies. Some studies have shown a correlation—though not yet causation—between geomagnetic spikes and unusual reports of spiritual or anomalous experiences.

It's not conclusive. But it's compelling. The brain is an electrochemical organ, after all. If our bodies respond to magnetic resonance in medical imaging, it stands to reason that strong natural variations might exert more subtle effects.

What I wanted—what I still want, if I'm honest—is to create a controlled study that doesn't just track these environmental factors after the fact, but maps them in real time alongside witness perception.

Imagine deploying sensors in a location long before anyone arrives. Measure the baseline—light, pressure, EM field, temperature, infrasound, geomagnetic data—all logged continuously. Then bring in volunteers, blind to the site's reputation, and document what they feel, see, or hear. Correlate their experiences with the environment's behavior. Look for patterns. Test those patterns in multiple locations.

The idea isn't to prove or disprove the paranormal. It is to clarify the boundaries of perception—to draw a clearer line between what's happening out there and what's happening in here, inside the body and brain. Because so many of the experiences people describe aren't evidence of external forces.

They're evidence of how profoundly the environment shapes what we think we know.

That study never happened. But I still believe it could. And if it did, it might change the entire conversation. Not by debunking belief—but by understanding its context and maybe filtering out the cases with natural causes.

AI ANALYSIS

If there's one area I never got to explore—simply because the tools didn't exist yet—it's the role artificial intelligence could play in analyzing paranormal data.

When I was most active in the field, AI wasn't something hobbyists or independent researchers could realistically harness. Machine learning was confined to university labs and tech giants. Today, it's everywhere. And part of me can't help but wonder what we might have uncovered if we'd had access to that kind of power just a decade or two earlier.

Pattern recognition has always been the missing piece in paranormal investigation. We talk endlessly about repeat phenomena—similar reports in similar locations, emotional responses that align, mechanical failures that defy explanation—but very little of it is ever captured in a way that could be meaningfully analyzed. Most data collected during investigations is anecdotal, disorganized, or riddled with confirmation bias. The sheer volume of noise—figurative and literal—makes it nearly impossible to draw conclusions without some kind of analytic aid. AI, especially modern machine learning models, thrives in that noise.

It doesn't need a dramatic incident. It doesn't care about the narrative. It just looks for patterns—statistical consistencies that emerge when you give it enough data.

I imagine now, what it would be like to take the thousands of hours of audio, environmental readings, infrared footage, and anecdotal reports I've accumulated and feed it all into a trained system. Let the machine cross-reference temperature drops with humidity shifts. Let it compare magnetometer readings across unrelated locations. Let it analyze language patterns in witness testimony—tone, cadence, stress levels— and flag subtle consistencies we never thought to look for.

None of that was feasible when I was actively investigating. The technology didn't exist at the scale or cost I could access. Even basic signal processing was a manual task. I spent hours scrolling through spectrograms frame by frame, trying to distinguish real structure from random interference. Today, a trained neural network could do that work in seconds—and it wouldn't be exhausted at the end.

Of course, AI isn't a silver bullet. It still needs clean data. It still needs clear definitions, consistent tagging, and thoughtful oversight. Garbage in, garbage out. But had the technology been available, I would have built an entire platform around it. A centralized, structured data repository where researchers could upload logs, tag events, and let the algorithms find what we so often miss. Not ghosts. But patterns.

That's where the real mystery lies—not in the shadows, but in the space between stories. In the coincidences too subtle for us to recognize, but too frequent to dismiss. That's the kind of work AI could help us do now. And sometimes I wonder if, had it arrived just a little sooner, I might have stayed in the field longer.

OMITTED GEAR AND METHODS

Looking back, what strikes me most isn't the equipment we used—it's the equipment we never used. The protocols we never adopted. The science we never even attempted.

For a field so obsessed with the unknown, paranormal investigation remains remarkably resistant to the known. The scientific method, with its insistence on control, repeatability, and falsifiability, was always just outside the room—nodded at, perhaps, but rarely invited inside. And yet, that's where the real missed opportunities lie: in the tools and techniques of hard science that could have fundamentally reshaped the work, had anyone been willing to do the hard part.

Take control groups, for instance. The gold standard in experimental design. In medicine, in psychology, in physics—controls are how we separate noise from signal. But in ghost hunting? They're practically nonexistent. Very few teams ever created baseline recordings under normal, non-investigative conditions. Fewer still returned to those same locations multiple times, at varying hours and in different seasons, to measure how environmental conditions changed independent of any paranormal claim. Most investigations are one-offs. In and out in a night or two. Whatever happens becomes "*evidence*." But evidence of what? Without a control, it's impossible to say.

Blind testing is another glaring omission. In any serious field of research, it's standard practice to isolate the observer from the expected result. You don't let a participant know what stimulus they're supposed to detect. You don't let a researcher interact with the subject if the researcher's own expectations could skew the outcome. But paranormal investigators almost always know the stories before they arrive.

They know which rooms are "*active*." They know what past guests have claimed. And whether they realize it or not, that knowledge shapes everything—from where they set up their equipment to what they think they see.

Then there's the issue of replication—another pillar of scientific inquiry. If a result cannot be reproduced, it cannot be trusted. But how many investigations are ever replicated? How many teams revisit the same site, under the same conditions, using the same methodology, and compare notes? The answer is almost none. And it's not because they don't want to. It's because replication requires patience, precision, and discipline—and those things don't sell nearly as well as exhibition, and yet, the tools to do it right were always within reach.

THE TOOLS NO ONE USED

Paranormal researchers could have used environmental sensors that recorded data with exact timestamps and location tracking. They could have introduced randomized test conditions to prevent unintentional cues or influence during the investigation.

They could have implemented formal logging systems modeled after field science—complete with observer blinding, control environments, and statistical thresholds. But more often than not, they chose the shortcut. The flashier gear. The story that fit the narrative, and that's where the real mystery lives—not in what we couldn't detect, but in what we never bothered to try.

One of the most glaring gaps in paranormal investigation has always been acoustics. For a field so obsessed with sound—EVPs, whispers, knocks—it's remarkable how little of it is treated with acoustic discipline. Sound behaves according to predictable rules. It reflects, refracts, diffuses, and interferes in ways that can be measured and modeled.

With the right tools—a calibrated microphone array, a basic signal analyzer, and some knowledge of room modes—you could trace the source of a supposed voice down to the wall that reflected it. You could separate true signal from standing wave. But almost no one ever does.

Where were the impulse response tests? The echo maps? Even a basic frequency sweep could help explain why some rooms '*feel*' strange. Low-frequency sound waves—especially in older buildings—can create pressure zones that you don't hear, but definitely feel. That's not paranormal. That's just physics. Yet you could probably count on one hand the number of investigators who've ever taken the time to map a room's acoustic signature.

And what about radiation? Particle detectors, ion counters, photomultiplier tubes—none of these are exotic. They're standard tools in physics labs. But in ghost hunting? Virtually absent.

Occasionally you'll see a Geiger counter hauled in for dramatic effect, but rarely with any contextual knowledge of what background radiation should look like in a given space, or how to differentiate alpha from beta emissions. If spirits were somehow manifesting energy—light, heat, ion discharge—why weren't we using the instruments designed to detect such things?

The same can be said for thermal imaging. FLIR cameras became popular in the paranormal world, but almost no one used them correctly. Few understood emissivity or thermal reflectivity. Fewer still controlled for air drafts, HVAC patterns, or reflective surfaces. What was presented as "*cold spots*" were often just IR reflections off glass or polished wood.

With even a modest understanding of thermography, most of the so-called anomalies could have been explained before they were ever uploaded to YouTube. I guess the views were more attractive.

PSYCHOLOGY

Then there's psychology—the one science that absolutely should have been front and center from the start. We know perception is fallible. We know memory is reconstructive, not reproductive. We know stress, expectation, fatigue, and emotional priming can all influence what people report. And yet, nearly every paranormal investigation treats eyewitness accounts as reliable starting points. They're not. They're data points—useful only when supported by environmental context, not as standalone proof.

How many teams ever used a standardized psychological inventory to track participant mood before, during, and after an investigation? How many logged ambient CO_2 levels, which are known to affect cognition and emotion? How many controlled for group suggestion or priming effects? In my experience, almost none.

These weren't expensive methods. They weren't even that difficult. They just required a different mindset—one rooted in skepticism and systems thinking. But most investigators didn't want to study the effect. They wanted to feel the effect. And there's a chasm between those two impulses.

Looking back, I don't lament the things we didn't find. I lament the things we never looked for properly. The tools we ignored. The questions we didn't ask. Not because we couldn't—but because we didn't want to complicate the mystery with method. But mystery doesn't disappear when you study it carefully. It sharpens. It reveals its boundaries. And sometimes, when you have the right tools and the right discipline, it tells you something more interesting than a shadow ever could.

THE WORK THAT REMAINS

I never expected to have all the answers. Most of the time, I wasn't even sure I was asking the right questions. But if there's one thing I know for certain, it's that I walked away from this work with more unfinished ideas than completed ones.

What you've just read isn't a list of regrets—it's a list of roads not taken or completed. Concepts I believed in. Technologies I wanted to refine. Patterns and practices I thought were worth chasing. Some were cut short by time, others by cost, and others by the simple limitations of metaphorically working alone. But none of them were abandoned because they failed. They were abandoned because the real world, as it often does, moved faster than my resources could, and yet, I still believe every one of these ideas has value.

I believe someone should revisit Backster's theories—not to validate them blindly, but to test them properly, with controls and rigor and curiosity. I believe someone should develop that electric field grid, or something like it, and build a true environmental monitoring system that doesn't rely on blinking LEDs and pseudoscience. I believe infrasound, geomagnetism, and barometric drift deserve serious long-term study—especially in relation to how they shape perception. And I believe, more than anything, that the field would benefit from a cultural shift toward real science. Toward humility. Toward patience. Toward method over mythology. *And stop using those damn quack gadgets!*

There's nothing wrong with wanting to believe. That impulse is human. But belief alone has never been a substitute for understanding. If this work is going to evolve—if we're ever going to separate the noise from the signal—it's going to take more than passion and infrared cameras. It's going to take structure, standards, persistence, and maybe a little less theater.

I've stepped away from that chase, at least for now. Life pulled me in other directions, and the deeper I went into engineering and signal analysis, the harder it became to justify returning to a field that seemed more interested in affirmation than inquiry. But that doesn't mean the work has to stop.

The ideas are still here. The tools are more accessible than ever. And the mystery—whatever it is—hasn't gone anywhere. Whether it's electrical interference, psychological suggestion, or something we haven't yet named, there is still something happening at the edges of perception. And I still believe it's worth studying. Carefully. Critically. Without ego.

So if you're reading this and you're still in the field—still searching—consider picking up one of these threads. Build the device. Run the test. Share the data. Not for ratings. Not for clicks. But for the quiet possibility that truth, however elusive, is still out there waiting. Waiting for someone to ask the right question—and this time, to keep going long enough to hear the answer.

CHAPTER TWELVE

THE RIGHT WAY TO BE WRONG

Just like *"evidence"*, in the world of paranormal investigation, the term *"scientific"* is as overused as it is misunderstood. It's been spray-painted across team logos, stitched into jackets, and invoked in every shaky YouTube video claiming to have recorded a ghost. But despite its omnipresence, the word rarely means what it should. In most cases, it's a costume—worn like a lab coat at a Halloween party. Serious in appearance. Hollow underneath.

So in this final chapter, I'm setting aside the anecdotes and overt critiques to answer the question I've been asked more times than I can count: *"What does a true scientific paranormal investigation actually look like?"*

What follows isn't a ghost hunt. It's a framework—modeled on the phases of the scientific method: Observation, Hypothesis, Testing, Analysis, and Replication. When applied properly, this structure transforms belief into inquiry—and inquiry into something measurable.

OBSERVATION

The answer begins long before a flashlight cuts through the dark or a question is whispered into an empty room. It starts not with equipment, but with a plan—not a checklist, but a framework rooted in the scientific method: observation, hypothesis, testing, analysis, and—most importantly—replicability.

Too many investigations begin with assumptions. A family reports footsteps. A video circulates online. A team arrives, loaded with gear but light on skepticism, and the goal quietly shifts from finding out what's happening to proving what's already believed. That's not investigation. That's confirmation bias in costume.

A scientifically sound investigation starts with baseline observation—a thorough understanding of the environment before any claims are considered. Investigators first define the scope. What phenomena have been reported? Where? When? Under what conditions? These are not prompts for belief, but boundaries for study. Specificity matters. *"I saw a shadow in the hallway"* becomes *"At 9:30 p.m. on three occasions, an occupant reported seeing a dark shape near the northeast doorway."* No editorializing. Just data points.

Once the scope is defined, the environmental survey begins. Every measurable variable must be recorded: temperature, humidity, EM field levels, sound pressure, light levels, barometric pressure, and any cyclical influences like HVAC systems, nearby traffic patterns, or industrial noise. These readings are not taken once. They are logged over time. A single EM field spike means nothing without knowing whether it recurs nightly when the refrigerator compressor kicks on.

This is where most amateur investigations falter: they confuse novelty for anomaly. A creaking pipe heard for the first time is labeled "unexplained." A knock that doesn't happen again becomes "paranormal." But without a control— without knowing how the environment behaves under normal conditions—no deviation can be meaningfully interpreted.

Next comes equipment auditing. Tools used in paranormal investigations are often misunderstood, misused, or misrepresented. Each device should be tested prior to deployment. Not just for functionality, but for limitations. What is the sensitivity of that microphone? What frequencies are being filtered out by that infrared camera? What is the error margin on that temperature sensor, and how does it change with battery level? These aren't pedantic questions—they're the difference between evidence and noise.

After equipment is vetted and the baseline logged, the testing phase begins. But contrary to popular belief, this doesn't mean lights-out and ghost stories. A proper investigation includes controlled conditions. That means accounting for observer effects, minimizing contamination, and logging every variable. If someone hears a whisper at 2:14

a.m., investigators should know what devices were active, what signals were recorded, where each team member was located, and what external events may have occurred at the same time.

Most importantly, all testing must be repeatable. A single surprising result is not proof. It is the beginning of a question. Replication is where the difference between storytelling and science becomes stark. In a ghost story, the thrill comes from the singular moment—the photo you can't explain, the voice caught once on tape. In science, a finding that cannot be reproduced is a fluke. At best, it's a mistake. At worst, it's misrepresentation.

This is why a competent investigator doesn't hunt for ghosts. They search for patterns. They build tests that can be run again. The investigation becomes a slow burn of controlled trials, not a sprint toward spectacle. If a door slams "on its own," the investigator doesn't marvel—they test. They measure the airflow, level the floor, check the hinges, monitor for pressure changes, and if possible, recreate the event deliberately. If it can be recreated, it must be. If it can't, the result is logged—not as "*paranormal*," but as "*anomalous, unverified.*"

That difference matters. Language in this work carries weight. Words like proof, spirit, haunted, or entity are conclusions masquerading as descriptions. A true scientific investigator uses neutral terms. An unexplained fluctuation in EM field is not "*paranormal activity.*" It's an unexplained fluctuation in EM field. Anything more is speculation—and speculation, while useful in forming hypotheses, has no place in conclusions.

To preserve integrity, a well-run investigation also builds in blinding—a method borrowed from experimental psychology and clinical trials. Simply put: when an investigator doesn't know the expected result of a test, their bias is less likely to influence the outcome. For example, if a test involves playing random audio clips to check for EVP, the analyst reviewing those clips should not be told which ones came from *"active"* moments and which came from control conditions. If they consistently *"hear voices"* in the controls too, then the pattern is psychological, not paranormal.

Similarly, redundancy is key. Single data points prove little. If an infrared sensor registers a cold spot, but no other tool agrees, it's probably an error—or an artifact. But if temperature, infrared, and airflow sensors all correlate across time and space, then the anomaly has structure. Structure invites analysis. Analysis leads to conclusions. And conclusions—real conclusions—are earned, not assumed.

Perhaps the most overlooked element in any paranormal investigation is the human variable. People are inconsistent sensors. We hallucinate. We forget. We misattribute. We hear patterns in static and see faces in shadows. This is not a flaw in character—it's a feature of how human brains work. Any investigation that places experiential testimony above measurable data risks becoming little more than a séance with gadgets.

That doesn't mean witnesses are irrelevant. On the contrary, witness accounts are often the trigger for legitimate inquiry. But those accounts must be contextualized, not canonized. They form the outer boundary of the question—not the answer.

In a proper investigation, it's not enough to say, *"I saw something."* The investigator's role is to ask, *"Under what conditions could something like that appear—and be misperceived as something else?"*

HYPOTHESIS

Once the environment has been documented and the preliminary variables cataloged, the next step is not to chase ghosts, but to design experiments. And like any good experiment, those used in a paranormal investigation must begin with a falsifiable hypothesis. Not *"Are ghosts real?"*— that's philosophy, not science.

A better question might be: *"Does this room consistently exhibit unaccounted-for EM field spikes during specific intervals?"* Or *"Do witnesses report auditory anomalies more frequently in low-frequency ambient environments?"* These are questions that can be tested. Measured. Challenged. And that's the point. A good investigation does not protect an idea; it subjects it to failure. The more resistant the result is to being disproven, the more robust it becomes.

TESTING

This is also where environmental control separates serious investigation from dramatic playacting. A *"cold spot"* is only meaningful if the rest of the building has been monitored for airflow, insulation gaps, and HVAC anomalies. A door closing by itself only matters if every window has been checked for drafts, hinges tested for balance, and the incline of the floor measured. And most crucially: timing matters.

Any claim that an anomaly is *"repeating"* or *"attached to a specific time"* needs to be met with round-the-clock data logging. Not just presence in the building, but passive environmental tracking—set to record continuously for several days, if possible. This is the only way to distinguish between event-driven anomalies and incidental fluctuations.

ANALYSIS

False positives are the bane of serious inquiry. They come in many forms: electromagnetic interference from cell towers, reflections from infrared light sources, battery sag on unregulated devices, or even subtle seismic activity. A proper investigator anticipates these variables and builds in controls to catch them. For example, if audio recorders are used to detect anomalous sound, at least one should be placed in a sealed, sound-isolated control location. If a similar anomaly appears on both the active and control recordings, it's probably environmental noise—not evidence.

This kind of layered control requires patience, technical literacy, and a willingness to be wrong. Most of all, it requires humility—an admission that the universe doesn't owe you a result. The presence of unknowns doesn't automatically signal the presence of the paranormal. A door that closes when no one is around might be compelling to a homeowner—but to a scientist, it's a data point to be investigated, not a revelation to be broadcast. That's the other thing: publicity ruins objectivity.

The moment an investigator begins thinking in terms of *"what will sound impressive,"* the process is compromised. Investigations should not be driven by the need to entertain an audience, build a brand, or support a belief system. They should be driven by a hunger to understand something strange—and a discipline that prevents that hunger from becoming a hallucination.

A real investigation, then, is not exciting in the cinematic sense. It's slow. It's methodical. And it's often deeply boring. But truth, unlike entertainment, doesn't owe you a climax.

Any serious paranormal investigation must also confront one of the most persistent—and invisible—threats to its integrity: the observer effect.

In physics, the term refers to how the act of observation can alter the phenomenon being observed. In paranormal investigation, it takes on an even trickier form. It's not just that equipment may cause interference—it's that human presence and expectation can bend reality into suggestion. The brain, when primed, is an accomplice in its own deception. A creak becomes a footstep. A breeze becomes a breath. A shadow becomes a figure that wasn't there before.

This is why the design of the investigation must actively include bias mitigation strategies. At the most basic level, that means keeping team members unaware of specific claims. If an investigator walks into a room believing a woman was once murdered there, every creak or shift in air pressure risks being interpreted as her—as if the dead were waiting for the right backstory to make an entrance. To protect the data from these contaminations, serious investigators segment information. One team collects witness statements. Another designs and deploys equipment, blind to the reported phenomena. A third analyzes the results, comparing findings against both baseline data and control conditions—still without knowing the personal accounts.

This structure isn't bureaucratic—it's protective. Of the truth. Of the process. Of the investigation's credibility. Bias doesn't only enter through belief. It sneaks in through pattern-seeking behavior, one of the most fundamental quirks of the human brain. We look for familiar shapes, familiar rhythms. A distant knocking sound? It becomes three raps: one-two-three—just like in the movies. A flicker in the light? It becomes Morse code. The world is chaos, and we are storytelling animals. This tendency, useful in survival, is disastrous in an investigation where being wrong must always remain on the table.

This is where many self-proclaimed investigators falter. They treat a lack of evidence as failure. Or worse, as suppression. *"They say the ghosts don't want to perform tonight"*, as if scientific instruments were psychic dowsing rods that only work when spirits are cooperative. But in true scientific inquiry, a negative result is still a result.

If no anomalies are recorded, no patterns emerge, no unexplained data surfaces—that is not failure. That is a finding. It narrows the scope. It informs the larger body of knowledge. It makes future investigations more focused, more precise. And it reminds the team of a fundamental rule: the universe does not exist for our entertainment. It owes us nothing. Least of all, evidence.

The discipline to accept this—without reaching for mystical explanations, without anthropomorphizing devices or interpreting silence as significance—is what separates professional research from performative hobbyism. The true investigator does not chase results. They chase rigor.

They understand that being wrong, being unsure, and walking away empty-handed are not signs of weakness. They are signs you're doing it right.

At the heart of any legitimate investigation—paranormal or otherwise—is documentation. Not the kind that gets filtered through narration or edited for dramatic effect, but cold, disciplined, objective record-keeping. Because no matter how precise your instrumentation or how rigorous your testing, data without context is noise. Worse, it's ammunition for speculation.

Everything must be documented: equipment settings, room conditions, time stamps, personnel movements, device calibrations, error margins, even the weather. These details don't make for compelling television, but they are what elevate an investigation from amateur inquiry to a process worthy of peer review.

Each anomalous event should be paired with environmental logs: was the barometric pressure dropping? Was there nearby construction? Was there a spike in geomagnetic activity? Was a team member adjusting equipment in the next room? These questions can't be answered after the fact unless the groundwork is laid in real time.

Just as critical is the chain of custody. In legal and scientific settings, this refers to the documented and unbroken control over evidence. In paranormal research, the same concept applies: once data is collected—be it audio, video, or environmental logs—it must be protected from tampering, both accidental and intentional.

That means no deleting clips that "don't show anything." No adjusting contrast or equalization without noting exactly how and when it was done. No retroactive trimming of silence from recordings. If a clip is enhanced or filtered to reveal a possible anomaly, the raw file must remain archived, untouched, and available for comparison. If video is analyzed, the original timestamps must be preserved and cross-verified with equipment logs. And if data cannot be authenticated or its handling cannot be verified? It's discarded. No matter how compelling the contents.

This is one of the great divides between scientific investigators and sensationalists: transparency. A serious investigator welcomes scrutiny. Their process is replicable. Their tools are documented. Their results are available for re-analysis. They are not protective of their findings, because they understand that truth withstands pressure. Only lies and wishful thinking require insulation.

Transparency also means acknowledging limitations. Was the equipment off for a portion of the night? Was there a known calibration issue in one of the thermocouples? Were there moments where control conditions lapsed—where a door was left ajar, or team members overlapped roles?

These are not embarrassments. They are facts. And facts are the currency of real investigation. If conditions weren't ideal, say so. If a result was muddy, explain why. The goal is not perfection—it's honesty. And in a field built on uncertainty, honesty is the only true safeguard against delusion.

REPLICATION

Perhaps most importantly, investigations must be reproducible. If another team, using the same methods in the same environment under similar conditions, cannot replicate the results, then the results lose credibility. This doesn't invalidate the experience—but it reclassifies it. It moves it from the category of *"evidence"* into the quieter, less flashy realm of "inconclusive data." And that, in science, is still progress.

In recent years, technology has become the costume of credibility. Blink enough LEDs on a black plastic box, and it begins to look like science. But a light show is not a measurement. And the misuse of technology—often by those who least understand it—has become one of the most dangerous habits in paranormal investigation. This isn't just a matter of error. It's a matter of misleading the public.

Many so-called *"paranormal tools"* are marketed as if they detect ghosts, when in fact they detect nothing of the sort. Devices originally designed for entirely unrelated fields—radio frequency testers, stud finders, motion alarms—are repackaged with new decals and sold to ghost hunters at a premium. Their readings are poorly understood, rarely calibrated, and often interpreted through a lens of narrative, not data.

A serious investigator must be fluent in their tools. Not just in how to operate them, but in how they work—what they measure, what interferes with them, what they don't measure despite common assumptions. Every piece of equipment carries with it a burden of responsibility. If you don't understand the architecture of a sensor or the range of a detector, you're not measuring anything—you're playing dress-up in a lab coat.

Equally troubling is the widespread use of pseudo-scientific rituals. The act of calling out into the dark, asking questions of "*entities*," then waiting for a creak or a knock, has become synonymous with investigation. But this is not method—it's theater. A creak in response to a question is not communication. It is coincidence. And if an investigator doesn't build in safeguards to test that coincidence, then they are not gathering evidence. They are reinforcing their own bias, in real time, while pretending to collect data.

This sort of activity may feel harmless, but it isn't—not when it's presented to the public as legitimate research. Most investigations are conducted in private homes. Real families live in these spaces. People who are scared, vulnerable, sometimes desperate. Presenting them with "*evidence*" of spirits based on gadgetry and guesswork is not just irresponsible—it's unethical.

An investigator must never forget that they are not merely collecting data. They are shaping perception. Every word, every interpretation, carries weight. If you tell a homeowner their bedroom is haunted based on a fluctuating EM field reading or a knock on the wall, you may be planting an idea that will stay with them for the rest of their lives. You may be validating trauma. Or creating it.

Scientific investigation carries a duty of care—not just toward data, but toward people. To avoid harm. To speak with precision. To make clear the line between what is known, what is suspected, and what is unknown. And if you can't walk into someone's home with that level of humility, discipline, and ethical restraint, then you have no business being there at all.

No matter how much equipment is deployed or how carefully an environment is logged, one truth remains: the most fallible instrument in any investigation is the human brain.

We are not neutral observers. We are pattern-seeking, emotionally driven, meaning-making machines. We connect dots before they exist. We fill gaps with memories, emotions, and culturally shaped expectations. And in the absence of clear information, we tell ourselves stories. This isn't a flaw. It's survival. But it becomes a liability in investigation.

Consider auditory pareidolia—the phenomenon of hearing words in static or meaningless noise. It's the cornerstone of electronic voice phenomena, or EVP, which is still regarded by many investigators as the "*gold standard*" of spirit communication. But under controlled conditions, people regularly "*hear*" messages in randomized sound bursts, especially after being told what to listen for. This isn't proof of communication. It's proof of suggestibility.

Visual perception is no better. In low-light environments, peripheral vision is notoriously unreliable. Shadows seem to move. Stationary objects warp and shift. A curtain stirs in the breeze and appears to take form. When these effects are reported during emotionally heightened states—fear, grief, anxiety—they're often interpreted as paranormal encounters, even when every factor involved has a natural explanation. The solution isn't to ignore witness testimony. It's to contextualize it.

A proper investigation welcomes the input of other disciplines. Psychology, neurology, acoustics, architecture, electrical engineering—all bring tools and frameworks that help separate perception from phenomenon. An investigator who refuses to collaborate, who sees outside expertise as threatening or irrelevant, is not a researcher. They're a believer wearing a toolbelt.

This is why multidisciplinary teams are critical. A psychologist can help identify stress-induced hallucinations or trauma-based belief formation. An acoustical engineer can model how sound might travel through old ductwork or walls. A historian might explain why a room has a strange feel—not because of tragedy, but because of its original design or forgotten use. Layers of insight reduce the likelihood of error. They also restore humility to a process too often warped by ego and performance.

But it's not just about avoiding mistakes. It's about building resilience into the process. When multiple perspectives are consulted, and all converge on the same question—that's when an anomaly becomes truly worth studying. Not because we've run out of explanations, but because we've ruled them out responsibly.

And even then, the correct response is not to shout "*proof*" from the rooftops. It's to say, carefully and precisely: "*This event remains unexplained under current conditions. Further study is warranted.*" That sentence doesn't sell TV shows. But it holds up to scrutiny. Which is the point.

Because in this work, the goal is not to dazzle or frighten.

It's to understand what happened, why it happened, and whether it can happen again under controlled conditions. Anything less isn't research. It's ritual.

Perhaps the hardest thing to accept in paranormal investigation is the absence of resolution. After weeks of setup, logging, analysis, and cross-checking, most investigations end not with a revelation, but a shrug. The data is inconclusive. The anomalies are explainable. The truly strange moments resist correlation.

To some, this feels like failure. But to those who practice real science, it's the mark of progress. Because in a proper investigation, the goal is not to confirm belief—it's to test it. And testing means risking disproof. It means putting your most compelling ideas into the ring with the harshest standards and seeing what survives. Most don't. That's not discouraging. That's how we get closer to the truth. This is where intellectual honesty becomes more than a virtue. It becomes a requirement.

It means saying "*I don't know*" instead of inventing a theory to fill the silence. It means resisting the urge to soften a report to appease a client or dramatize a result for an audience. It means reminding yourself, again and again, that truth is not democratic—no amount of consensus, enthusiasm, or anecdotal evidence can transform a belief into a fact. This kind of rigor takes practice. It takes discipline. And it often means walking away empty-handed.

But there is meaning in the search itself. Every null result narrows the field. Every tested assumption sheds light on the way we perceive, the way we misinterpret, the way we need stories more than we need evidence. And that in itself is worthy of study.

A real investigation doesn't require flickering lights or voices from the void. It requires quiet. The kind of quiet where conclusions aren't rushing in to fill the gaps. Where doubt is allowed to breathe. Where questions remain questions, even when the temptation to answer them becomes overwhelming. And maybe—if anything in this field is to be taken seriously— it's that kind of quiet we should be seeking.

Because ghosts, if they exist, don't care whether we believe in them. But science demands that we don't believe in anything without evidence. So you check the floorboards. You map the air currents. You log the temperatures, calibrate the instruments, and double-blind your data analysis. You ask other experts. You challenge your findings. You publish your methodology.

And when the lights come on and you pack the cases and nothing truly strange has occurred—you do not rewrite the story to make it fit. You write it down honestly. And you move on to the next question. Because in the end, the work isn't about proving ghosts are real. It's about proving that you were willing to find out if they weren't.

EPILOGUE

MY FINAL THOUGHTS

When I finally stepped away from the field, I didn't do it because I'd stopped caring about the truth. I did it because I realized the truth didn't matter to everyone in the same way it mattered to me. For some, the "*truth*" was whatever story felt most satisfying in the moment. If the client wanted a haunted house, they got a haunted house. If they wanted a demon, someone would name one for them. That gap—between what's real and what's useful to say—is where the damage starts.

I've never expected hobbyist paranormal investigators to hold themselves to the same standards as a research physicist or a forensic engineer. We don't all have the funding, the training, or the time. But there is a bright line you cannot cross.

You cannot walk into someone's home, look them in the eye, and declare—as fact—that there is a malevolent force destined to harm them, without also accepting every ounce of the responsibility that such a claim demands.

Because when you say those words, you are no longer just a curious visitor with a K-II meter. You've made yourself an authority in that person's life. You've handed them a verdict that will shape how they sleep at night, how they explain every bump in the dark, and in some cases, how they make financial, medical, and emotional decisions. You've planted something that may grow into fear, obsession, or trauma. If you haven't built that conclusion on solid ground, you're gambling with someone else's well-being.

It is easy to forget how much weight your words carry when you've been in the field long enough. You stand in so many rooms, hear so many accounts, and you start to develop a script—the same reassurances, the same phrases you've heard others use. It becomes routine. And routine dulls your sense of consequence. But for the person hearing it for the first time— the family whose child won't sleep alone, the elderly widow who feels watched—those words can detonate.

I've seen it happen. I've seen the tears, the sleepless nights, the clients who spend thousands on "*cleansings*" and "*protections*" that no one can prove do anything. I've also seen the quiet damage: the erosion of trust in one's own senses, the belief that every misfortune has a supernatural cause, the slow, grinding anxiety that comes from thinking you're under attack by something you can't see. And I've seen that damage delivered by people who, in any other context, would admit they have no way to verify their claims.

So this is the line in the sand I wish the field would draw: curiosity is free, but authority is not. The moment you speak with certainty about the unseen, you've crossed into a role that demands evidence, rigor, and accountability. You can't have it both ways.

Some investigators push back when I say this. They tell me, "*But people call us because they want answers. They need to know what's going on.*" I agree. But there's a difference between giving them your best assessment and stamping that assessment as fact without the burden of proof. There's a difference between saying, "*We recorded some anomalies we can't explain,*" and "*You have a demon in your house.*"

The first statement invites the client to participate in the search for understanding. The second traps them inside your version of the story.

And once you've locked them in that story, you own the fallout. If that person stops sleeping in their bedroom because you told them a shadow figure lives there, that's on you. If their relationship strains under the constant stress of "*entity activity,*" that's on you. If they sink into fear, paranoia, or despair because they believe something inhuman is hunting them—you built that belief. You may not be there to see the damage, but it doesn't mean it isn't happening.

Here's what's often forgotten: you are walking into the most intimate spaces of someone's life—their home, their memories, their fears—at a time when they feel vulnerable. That is not a stage. It is not an episode of television. It is someone's lived reality. Treating it like entertainment is not only unprofessional; it's unethical.

When you claim to know something about their situation—especially something frightening—you take on a responsibility whether you like it or not. You can't shrug that off later with "*Well, I'm not a scientist.*" The minute you present yourself as someone who understands "*the paranormal*" more than they do, you've claimed authority. And authority, in any context, comes with rules.

If you're going to play that role, you must earn it. That means collecting evidence with real controls, understanding your tools beyond their blinking lights, and being willing to accept that the most honest answer might be "*I don't know.*" It means resisting the urge to dress up maybes as certainties, because certainties in this field are very, very rare.

The hard truth is that much of what passes for "paranormal evidence" today would collapse under the simplest scientific scrutiny. Temperature fluctuations, EMF spikes, spirit box chatter—most of it can be explained without invoking the supernatural. That doesn't mean the client's experiences aren't real. It means the explanation might be something we don't yet understand, and that "*unknown*" is a more accurate—and more responsible—label than "*demonic.*"

Unfortunately, "*unknown*" doesn't sell T-shirts. It doesn't drive YouTube subscribers. It doesn't fill seats at conventions. And so, over and over, the field rewards the people willing to offer the loudest, most dramatic answer, even when it's the least defensible. But if you care about the truth—and about the people who trust you—you have to resist that reward.

If you've never watched someone unravel under the weight

of a paranormal "*diagnosis*," count yourself lucky. I have. I've seen families who were merely uneasy about their home become terrified to live in it after an investigator assured them they were dealing with a malevolent presence. I've seen parents who once dismissed their child's bad dreams now panic at every noise in the hallway because a visiting team told them, point-blank, "*You have a demon here!*"

And here's the part that still bothers me the most: those same investigators will often leave with high-fives and grins, feeling like they've given the client something exciting. In reality, they've just dropped a live grenade into someone's life and walked away.

It's easy to forget that fear isn't a static thing. Once planted, it grows. The homeowner who hears a pop in the attic doesn't just hear a pop anymore—they hear the beginning of an attack. The creak of settling floorboards becomes a warning. A flicker in the light becomes a signal. Everyday noises stop being everyday. That's not "*help*." That's indoctrination into a worldview they didn't ask for, and one they may never be able to fully unlearn.

You might think, "*Well, if they called me, they already believed something was wrong.*" That's true. But belief is a spectrum. When you enter someone's life with your gadgets and your confidence, you can push them deeper into that belief—or you can help them navigate it with perspective. The difference is in how you frame your findings.

If your goal is to leave them informed and empowered, then your conclusions must be supported by something more than gut feeling or dramatic effect. If your goal is simply to give them a thrill or a scare, then you're in the wrong business, because this is not a business built on the harmless. People have taken their own lives over fears of spiritual attack. People have abandoned homes, drained savings, and cut ties with loved ones over ideas planted by investigators who never stopped to ask themselves whether they could back up their claims.

This is why I push so hard on the idea that you can't have it both ways. You can't claim the authority of a specialist—the one who "knows" what's going on—and at the same time disclaim the obligations that come with that authority. You can't operate with the credibility of a doctor and the accountability of a hobbyist.

If you want to keep it casual, then keep your language casual. Say, *"We noticed some unusual readings, but we can't say for sure what they mean."* Say, *"We experienced a few things we couldn't immediately explain."* That is honest. That is safe. That leaves room for more investigation without cementing fear into the walls.

But if you choose to speak in absolutes—if you tell a family that their home is cursed, that their child is being stalked by a dark entity, that they are living alongside something *"evil"*— then you have crossed into a level of influence that demands education, verification, and restraint. Anything less is recklessness disguised as expertise.

The paranormal field doesn't have a licensing board. There's no governing body to revoke your credentials if you get it wrong, no ethics committee to review your claims, no malpractice insurance when you cause harm. That's exactly why the responsibility has to come from you. Because no one else is going to hold you to a standard—and too many will cheer you on for ignoring one.

It's tempting to think of this work as harmless curiosity. For some cases, maybe it is. But the moment your words alter someone's sense of safety in their own home, you've stepped into something far heavier. Whether you meant to or not, you've shaped their reality. You've told them how to interpret every creak, flicker, and shadow from now on. You've placed yourself in the role of interpreter between them and the unknown. That is not casual. That is not entertainment. That is influence.

Influence is power, and power always comes with a cost. If you don't believe me, ask yourself this: would you stake your own family's peace of mind, your own financial security, your own sleep, on the strength of the evidence you just presented to someone else? If the answer is no, then you had no business delivering it as truth.

This is the part that I hope sticks with anyone still working in the field: you can be curious without being careless. You can investigate without inflating. You can share your findings honestly, even when they're inconclusive, and still earn trust. In fact, you'll earn more of it—because the people you're serving will know you're not there to sell them a story. You're there to help them see their own situation as clearly as possible.

That clarity is worth far more than a thrilling conclusion. A client who understands that the cause of their fear is still undetermined has options. They can continue looking for answers. They can explore environmental or psychological causes. They can weigh possibilities without feeling doomed by an *"expert verdict"* that might not hold up to the smallest bit of scrutiny.

The truth is, there will always be those in this field who build their identity on certainty, because certainty sells. But for the rest of us—the ones who understand the cost of getting it wrong—there's a different kind of legacy worth building. One that prizes restraint over drama, honesty over mystique, and the long-term well-being of clients over the short-term rush of a "gotcha" moment.

You don't have to be a scientist to follow scientific principles. You don't need a degree to uphold ethical responsibility. But you do need to understand the weight of your words—and the line between exploring the unknown and exploiting it. Cross that line, and you're not just chasing ghosts anymore. You're creating them. And you'll have to live with that, whether they're real or not.

So be curious. Be thorough. Be humble. And above all, be accountable. Because you can't have it both ways.

"The great tragedy of Science—the slaying of a beautiful hypothesis by an ugly fact."

Thomas H. Huxley

This QR code connects you to a collection of my projects—original music, books, and products I've created. I invite you to explore and enjoy what I've been working on.

https://lynktu.com/Michael/Projects